Loot

Loot was Joe Orton's second play to be staged. It was first produced in London in 1966 by the London Traverse Theatre Company. The play makes use of all the apparatus of 'strong drama' – crime and violence, pious sentiments and ironic coincidences, mystery and its labyrinthine elucidation, illicit passions and the solemn trappings of death. But from this gaunt skeleton burgeons a fantastic and luxuriant growth of such hilarity that it took audiences and critics, in spite of themselves, by storm.

'*Loot* establishes Mr Orton's niche in English drama. He is the Oscar Wilde of Welfare State gentility.'
Ronald Bryden in *The Observer*

'The most genuinely quick-witted, pungent and sprightly entertainment by a new, young British playwright for a decade . . .'
Alan Brien in the *Sunday Telegraph*

The photograph on the front cover shows a scene from the London Traverse production and is reproduced by courtesy of John Haynes

by the same author

*

ENTERTAINING MR SLOANE
CRIMES OF PASSION

LOOT

Joe Orton

LONDON
METHUEN & CO LTD
11 NEW FETTER LANE EC4

First published 1967
Reprinted 1968
© *1967 by Joe Orton*

S.B.N. 416 11470 9 pb
S.B.N. 416 11440 7 hb

Printed in Great Britain by
W & J Mackay & Co Ltd
Chatham

To
PEGGY

LORD SUMMERHAYS. Anarchism is a game at which the Police can beat you. What have you to say to that?

GUNNER. What have I to say to it! Well I call it scandalous: that's what I have to say to it.

LORD SUMMERHAYS. Precisely: that's all anybody has to say to it, except the British Public, which pretends not to believe it.

Misalliance George Bernard Shaw

The first London production of LOOT *was given at the Jeanetta Cochrane Theatre by the London Traverse Theatre Company on 29 September 1966, with the following cast:*

MCLEAVY	Gerry Duggan
FAY	Sheila Ballantine
HAL	Kenneth Cranham
DENNIS	Simon Ward
TRUSCOTT	Michael Bates
MEADOWS	David Redmond

Directed by Charles Marowitz

Designed by Tony Carruthers

Act One

A room in MCLEAVY'S *house. Afternoon.*
Door left with glass panel. Door right. A coffin stands on trestles. MCLEAVY, *in mourning, sits beside an electric fan.*
FAY, *in a nurse's uniform, enters from the left.*

FAY. Wake up. Stop dreaming. The cars will be here soon. (*She sits.*) I've bought you a flower.
MCLEAVY. That's a nice thought. (*Taking the flower from her.*)
FAY. I'm a nice person. One in a million.

She removes her slippers, puts on a pair of shoes.

MCLEAVY. Are those Mrs McLeavy's slippers?
FAY. Yes. She wouldn't mind my having them.
MCLEAVY. Is the fur genuine?
FAY. It's fluff, not fur.
MCLEAVY. It looks like fur.
FAY. (*standing to her feet*). No. It's a form of fluff. They manufacture it in Leeds.

She picks up the slippers and takes them to the wardrobe. She tries to open the wardrobe. It is locked. She puts the slippers down.

You realize, of course, that the death of a patient terminates my contract?
MCLEAVY. Yes.
FAY. When do you wish me to leave?
MCLEAVY. Stay for a few hours. I've grown used to your company.

FAY. Impossible. I'm needed at other sickbeds. Complain to the Society if you disagree with the rules.

She picks up his coat, holds it out for him to put on.

You've been a widower for three days. Have you considered a second marriage yet?

MCLEAVY (*struggling into his coat*). No.

FAY. Why not?

MCLEAVY. I've been so busy with the funeral.

FAY. You must find someone to take Mrs McLeavy's place. She wasn't perfect.

MCLEAVY. A second wife would be a physical impossibility.

FAY. I'll hear none of that. My last husband at sixty came through with flying colours. Three days after our wedding he was performing extraordinary feats.

She takes the coathanger to the wardrobe. She tries to open the wardrobe door, frowns, puts the coathanger beside her slippers.

You must marry a girl with youth and vitality. Someone with a consistent attitude towards religion. That's most important. With her dying breath Mrs McLeavy cast doubt upon the authenticity of the Gospels. What kind of wife is that for you? The leading Catholic layman within a radius of forty miles. Where did you meet such a woman?

MCLEAVY. At an informal get-together run by a Benedictine monk.

FAY *takes the flower from his hand and pins it on to his coat.*

FAY. Was she posing as a Catholic?

MCLEAVY. Yes.

FAY. She had a deceitful nature. That much is clear. We mustn't let it happen again. I'll sort out some well-meaning young woman. Bring her here. Introduce you. I can visualize her – medium height, slim, fair hair. A regular visitor to

some place of worship. And an ex-member of the League of
Mary.

MCLEAVY. Someone like yourself?

FAY. Exactly. (*She takes a clothes brush and brushes him down.*)
Realize your potential. Marry at once.

MCLEAVY. St Kilda's would be in uproar.

FAY. The Fraternity of the Little Sisters is on my side.
Mother Agnes-Mary feels you're a challenge. She's treating
it as a specifically Catholic problem.

MCLEAVY. She treats washing her feet as a Catholic problem.

FAY. She has every right to do so.

MCLEAVY. Don't Protestants have feet then?

FAY. The Holy Father hasn't given a ruling on the subject and
so, as far as I'm concerned, they haven't. Really, I sometimes
wonder whether living with that woman hasn't made a free
thinker of you. You must marry again after a decent interval
of mourning.

MCLEAVY. What's a decent interval?

FAY. A fortnight would be long enough to indicate your grief.
We must keep abreast of the times.

She takes the brush to the wardrobe and tries to open it.

(*Turning, with a frown.*) Who has the key to this cupboard?

MCLEAVY. Harold.

FAY. Why is it locked?

MCLEAVY. He refused to give a reason.

MCLEAVY *shakes the wardrobe door.*

FAY. Your son is a thorn in my flesh. The contents of his
dressing-table are in indictment of his way of life. Not only
firearms, but family-planning equipment. A Papal dispensa-
tion is needed to dust his room.

She goes out left. MCLEAVY *follows her. She can be heard
calling:*

(*Off.*) Harold! (*Farther off.*) Harold!

> HAL *enters right. He goes to the wardrobe, unlocks it, looks in, and locks the wardrobe again. He stands beside the coffin and crosses himself.* FAY *and* MCLEAVY *re-enter left.*

FAY (*pause, with a smile*). Why is the wardrobe locked?

HAL. I've personal property in there.

MCLEAVY. Open the door. There's enough mystery in the universe without adding to it.

HAL. I can't. You wouldn't wish to see. It's a present for your anniversary.

MCLEAVY. What anniversary?

HAL. Your being made a knight of the Order of St Gregory.

MCLEAVY. I'm not convinced. Open the wardrobe.

HAL. No.

FAY (*to* MCLEAVY). You see how far things have progressed? Your son won't obey you. (*To* HAL.) Are you still refusing to attend your mother's funeral?

HAL. Yes.

FAY. What excuse do you give?

HAL. It would upset me.

FAY. That's exactly what a funeral is meant to do.

MCLEAVY. He prefers to mourn in private.

FAY. I'm not in favour of private grief. Show your emotions in public or not at all.

HAL (*to* MCLEAVY). Another wreath has arrived.

MCLEAVY. Is it roses?

HAL. Roses and fern.

MCLEAVY. I must look.

> *He goes out left.*

FAY. I sometimes think your father has a sentimental attachment to roses.

HAL. Do you know what his only comment was on my mother's death?

FAY. Something suitable, I'm sure.

She takes the mattress cover from the mattress and folds it.

HAL. He said he was glad she'd died at the right season for
roses. He's been up half the night cataloguing the varieties
on the crosses. You should've seen him when that harp
arrived. Sniffing the petals, checking, arguing with the man
who brought it. They almost came to blows over the pro-
nunciation.

FAY *hangs the folded mattress cover over the screen.*

If she'd played her cards right, my mother could've cited
the Rose Growers' Annual as co-respondent.

FAY. The Vatican would never grant an annulment. Not unless
he'd produced a hybrid.

HAL (*at the coffin, looking in*). Why was she embalmed?

FAY. She asked to be scientifically preserved after her last
attack.

HAL *stares into the coffin, deep in thought.* FAY *joins him.*

You couldn't wish her life. She was in agony since Easter.

HAL. Yes, the egg I presented to her went untouched.

FAY. On doctor's orders, I can tell you in confidence.

Pause.

Sit down, Harold. I want a word with you. Your father can't
be expected to help at the moment.

HAL *sits.* FAY *sits opposite him.*

(*Folding her hands in her lap.*) The priest at St Kilda's has
asked me to speak to you. He's very worried. He says you
spend your time thieving from slot machines and deflowering
the daughters of better men than yourself. Is this a fact?

HAL. Yes.

FAY. And even the sex you were born into isn't safe from your marauding. Father Mac is popular for the remission of sins, as you know. But clearing up after you is a full-time job. He simply cannot be in the confessional twenty-four hours a day. That's reasonable, isn't it? You do see his point?

HAL. Yes.

FAY. What are you going to do about this dreadful state of affairs?

HAL. I'm going abroad.

FAY. That will please the Fathers. Who are you going with?

HAL. A mate of mine. Dennis. A very luxurious type of lad. At present employed by an undertaker. And doing well in the profession.

FAY. Have you known him long?

HAL. We shared the same cradle.

FAY. Was that economy or malpractice?

HAL. We were too young then to practise, and economics still defeat us.

FAY. You've confirmed my worst fears. You have no job. No prospects. And now you're about to elope to the Continent with a casual acquaintance and not even a baby as justification. Where will you end? Not respected by the world at large like your father. Most people of any influence will ignore you. You'll be forced to associate with young men like yourself. Does that prospect please you?

HAL. I'm not sure.

FAY. Well, hesitation is something to be going on with. We can build on that. What will you do when you're old?

HAL. I shall die.

FAY. I see you're determined to run the gamut of all experience. That can bring you nothing but unhappiness. You've had every chance to lead a decent life and rejected them. I've no further interest in your career. (*She rises to her feet.*) Call your father. He's surely had enough of the company of plants for the present.

HAL *goes to the door left.*

HAL (*calling*). Eh, Dad!

FAY. Shhh! This is a house of mourning.

HAL *returns and sits.*

The priest that came to pay his condolences had such quiet tones that at first I thought they'd sent along a mute.

MCLEAVY *enters carrying a large wreath marked off into numbered squares.*

MCLEAVY. The Friends of Bingo have sent a wreath. The blooms are breathtaking.

He puts the wreath down. Sits. Takes out a newspaper. FAY, *standing beside the coffin, looking into it, silently moves her lips in prayer, a rosary between her fingers.*

(*With a loud exclamation.*) Another catastrophe has hit the district! Bank robbers have got away with a fortune.

FAY (*looking up*). Which bank?

MCLEAVY. Next door to the undertakers. They burrowed through. Filled over twenty coffins with rubble.

FAY. Rubble?

MCLEAVY. From the wall. Demolished the wall, they did.

FAY. People are so unbalanced these days. The man sitting next to you on the bus could be insane.

MCLEAVY. Where the money has gone is still occupying the police. It's one of the big gangs, I expect.

HAL. What do you known of the big gangs? It's a small gang. Minute.

FAY. Do you know the men concerned?

HAL. If I had that money, I wouldn't be here. I'd go away.

FAY. You're going away.

HAL. I'd go away quicker.

FAY. Where would you go?

HAL. Spain. The playground of international crime.

FAY. Where are you going?

HAL. Portugal.

Pause.

You'll have to get up early in the morning to catch me.

Door chimes. HAL *goes to the window, draws back the curtains and looks out.*

Dennis is here with the cars.

FAY. Is he driving?

HAL. Yes. He looks impressive. Close proximity to death obviously agrees with him.

He goes out left.

MCLEAVY (*putting away the newspaper*). What's the plan for the afternoon?

FAY. The funeral will occupy you for an hour or so. Afterwards a stroll to the house of a man of God, a few words of wisdom and a glance through the Catholic Truth Society's most recent publication should set your adrenalin flowing. Then a rest. I don't want you overstrained.

MCLEAVY. When did you say you were leaving? I don't wish to cause you any inconvenience.

FAY. I'll decide when you've inconvenienced me long enough.

MCLEAVY. You're very good to me.

FAY. As long as you appreciate my desire to help. My own life has been unhappy. I want yours to be different.

MCLEAVY. You've had an unhappy life?

FAY. Yes. My husbands died. I've had seven altogether. One a year on average since I was sixteen. I'm extravagant you see. And then I lived under stress near Penzance for some time. I've had trouble with institutions. Lack of funds. A court case with my hairdresser. I've been reduced to asking people for money before now.

MCLEAVY. Did they give it to you?

FAY. Not willingly. They had to be persuaded. (*With a bright smile.*) I shall accompany you to your lawyers. After the reading of your wife's will you may need skilled medical assistance.

MCLEAVY (*with a laugh*). I don't think there are any surprises in store. After a few minor bequests the bulk of Mrs McLeavy's fortune comes to me.

FAY. I've also arranged for your doctor to be at your side. You've a weak heart.

> DENNIS *enters left.*

DENNIS. Good afternoon. I don't want to be too formal on this sad occasion, but would you like to view the deceased for the last time?

> FAY *takes out a handkerchief.*
> HAL *enters.*

(*To* HAL.) Give us a hand into the car with the floral tributes.

> HAL *takes out several wreaths,* DENNIS *picks up the rest.*

(*To* FAY.) We'll need help with the coffin. (*Nods to* MC-LEAVY.) He's too near the grave himself to do much lifting.

FAY. Harold can carry his mother to the car.

DENNIS. A charming suggestion. (*To* MCLEAVY.) If you'll be making your last good-byes while I give them a hand?

> *Takes the wreaths to the door.* HAL *enters left.*

(*Passing* HAL *in the doorway.*) I want a word with you.

> DENNIS *goes out left.* HAL *is about to follow him.*

FAY (*calling*). Come and see your mother, Harold. You'll never see her again.

MCLEAVY, HAL *and* FAY *stand beside the coffin, looking in.*

She looks a treat in her W.V.S uniform. Though I'd not care to spend Eternity in it myself.

HAL. She's minus her vital organs, isn't she?

FAY. It's a necessary part of the process.

MCLEAVY. Where are they?

FAY. In the little casket in the hall. Such tranquillity she has. Looks as though she might speak.

MCLEAVY (*taking out a handkerchief, dabbing his nose*). God rest the poor soul. I shall miss her.

FAY. Death can be very tragic for those who are left.

They bow their heads in silence.

HAL. Here, her eyes are blue. Mum's eyes were brown. That's a bit silly, isn't it?

FAY. I expect they ran out of materials.

MCLEAVY. Are her eyes not natural, then?

FAY. No. (*With a smile, to* HAL.) He's such an innocent, isn't he? Not familiar with the ways of the world.

MCLEAVY. I thought they were her own. That surprises me. Not her own eyes.

DENNIS *enters with a screwdriver.*

DENNIS. The large harp we've placed on top of the motor. On the coffin we thought just the spray of heather from her homeland.

MCLEAVY. It's going to take me a long time to believe she's dead. She was such an active sort of person.

FAY (*to* DENNIS). You're going abroad, I hear?

DENNIS. Yes.

FAY. Where did you get the money?

DENNIS. My life insurance has matured.

MCLEAVY (*to* DENNIS). Tragic news about your premises. Was the damage extensive?

DENNIS. The repair bill will be steep. We're insured, of course.

MCLEAVY. Was your Chapel of Rest defiled?

DENNIS. No.

MCLEAVY. Human remains weren't outraged?

DENNIS. No.

MCLEAVY. Thank God for that. There are some things which deter even criminals.

DENNIS. I'm concerned with the actual furnishings damaged – I mean, the inside of the average casket is a work of art – time and labour, oh, it makes you weep.

MCLEAVY. The bodies laid out. Waiting for burial. It's terrible thoughts that come to me.

DENNIS. It broke my heart. Dust and rubble.

MCLEAVY. What a terrible thing to contemplate. The young men, thinking only of the money, burrowing from the undertakers to the bank. The smell of corruption and the instruments of death behind them, the riches before them. They'd do anything for money. They'd risk damnation in this world and the next for it. And me, a good man by any lights, moving among such people. They'll have it on their conscience. Even if they aren't caught, they'll suffer.

DENNIS. How?

MCLEAVY. I don't know. But such people never benefit from their crimes. It's people like myself who have the easy time. Asleep at nights. Despite appearances to the contrary, criminals are poor sleepers.

FAY. How do you sleep, Harold?

HAL. Alone.

DENNIS. We'll be leaving in a short time, Mr McLeavy. I'd like to satisfy myself that everything is as it should be. We pride ourselves on the service.

MCLEAVY. What clothes would they wear, d'you suppose? Dust is easily identified. They'd surely not work in the nude? God have mercy on them if they did. Even to avoid the hangman I'd not put up with precautions of that nature.

FAY. They'd wear old clothes. Burn them after.

MCLEAVY. If you could get a glance between their toes you'd find the evidence. But to order a man to remove his clothes isn't within the power of the police. More's the pity, I say. I'd like to see them given wider powers. They're hamstrung by red tape. They're a fine body of men. Doing their job under impossible conditions.

HAL. The police are a lot of idle buffoons, Dad. As you well know.

MCLEAVY. If you ever possess their kindness, courtesy and devotion to duty, I'll lift my hat to you.

DENNIS. I'm going to batten down the hatches now.

MCLEAVY (*glancing into the coffin*). Treat her gently. She was very precious to me.

He goes out left.

FAY (*following* MCLEAVY, *turning in the doorway*). I'll be consoling your father if I'm needed. Be careful what you talk about in front of the dead.

She goes out left.
DENNIS *opens a packet of chewing-gum, puts a piece in his mouth, takes off his hat.*

DENNIS. Lock the door.

HAL. It won't lock.

DENNIS. Put a chair under the handle. We're in trouble

HAL wedges a chair under the handle.

We've had the law round our house.

HAL. When?

DENNIS. This morning. Knocked us up they did. Turning over every bleeding thing.

HAL. Was my name mentioned?

DENNIS. They asked me who my associate was. I swore blind

I never knew what they were on about. 'Course, it's only a
matter of time before they're round here.

HAL. How long?

DENNIS. Might be on their way now. (*He begins to screw down
the lid of the coffin.*) Don't want a last squint, do you? No?
Where's the money?

HAL taps the wardrobe.

In there? All of it? We've got to get it away. I'll lose faith
in us if we get nicked again. What was it last time?

HAL. Ladies' overcoats.

DENNIS. See? Painful. Oh, painful. We were a laughing-stock
in criminal circles. Banned from that club with the spade
dancer.

HAL. Don't go on, baby. I remember the humiliating circumstances of failure.

DENNIS. We wouldn't have been nicked if you'd kept your
mouth shut. Making us look ridiculous by telling the truth.
Why can't you lie like a normal man?

HAL. I can't, baby. It's against my nature.

He stares at the coffin as DENNIS screws the lid down.

Has anybody ever hidden money in a coffin?

DENNIS looks up. Pause.

DENNIS. Not when it was in use.

HAL. Why not?

DENNIS. It's never crossed anybody's mind.

HAL. It's crossed mine.

*He takes the screwdriver from DENNIS, and begins to un-
screw the coffin lid.*

It's the comics I read. Sure of it.

DENNIS (*wiping his forehead with the back of his hand*). Think of
your mum. Your lovely old mum. She gave you birth.

HAL. I should thank anybody for that?

DENNIS. Cared for you. Washed your nappies. You'd be some kind of monster.

HAL takes the lid off the coffin.

HAL. Think what's at stake.

He goes to wardrobe and unlocks it.

Money.

He brings out the money. DENNIS *picks up a bundle of notes, looks into the coffin.*

DENNIS. Won't she rot it? The body juices? I can't believe it's possible.

HAL. She's embalmed. Good for centuries.

DENNIS *puts a bundle of notes into the coffin. Pause. He looks at* HAL.

DENNIS. There's no room.

HAL lifts the corpse's arm.

HAL (*pause, frowns*). Remove the corpse. Plenty of room then.

DENNIS. Seems a shame really. The embalmers have done a lovely job.

They lift the coffin from the trestles.

There's no name for this, is there?

HAL. We're creating a precedent. Into the cupboard. Come on.

They tip the coffin on end and shake the corpse into the wardrobe. They put the coffin on the floor, lock the wardrobe and begin to pack the money into the coffin.

DENNIS. What will we do with the body?

HAL. Bury it. In a mineshaft. Out in the country. Or in the marshes. Weigh the corpse with rock.

DENNIS. We'll have to get rid of that uniform.

HAL (*pause*). Take her clothes off?

DENNIS. In order to avoid detection should her remains be discovered.

HAL. Bury her naked? My own mum?

He goes to the mirror and combs his hair.

It's a Freudian nightmare.

DENNIS (*putting lid upon coffin*). I won't disagree.

HAL. Aren't we committing some kind of unforgivable sin?

DENNIS. Only if you're a Catholic.

HAL (*turning from the mirror*). I am a Catholic. (*Putting his comb away.*) I can't undress her. She's a relative. I can go to Hell for it.

DENNIS. I'll undress her then. I don't believe in Hell.

He begins to screw down the coffin lid.

HAL. That's typical of your upbringing, baby. Every luxury was lavished on you – atheism, breast-feeding, circumcision. I had to make my own way.

DENNIS. We'll do it after the funeral. Your dad'll be with the priest.

HAL. O.K. And afterwards we'll go to a smashing brothel I've just discovered. Run by a woman who was connected with the Royal Family one time. Very ugly bird. Part Polish. Her eyes look that way. Nice line in crumpet she has. (*He sits astride the coffin.*)

DENNIS. I can't go to a brothel.

HAL. Why not?

DENNIS. I'm on the wagon. I'm trying to get up sufficient head of steam to marry.

HAL. Have you anyone in mind?

DENNIS. Your mum's nurse.

HAL. She's older than you.

DENNIS. An experienced woman is the finest thing that can happen to a lad. My dad swears by them.

HAL. She's three parts Papal nuncio. She'd only do it at set times.

DENNIS. Oh, no. She does it at any time. A typical member of the medical profession she is.

HAL. You've had her? (DENNIS *grins.*) Knocked it off? Really?

DENNIS. Under that picture of the Sacred Heart. You've seen it?

HAL. In her room. Often.

DENNIS. On Wednesday nights while you're training at St Edmund's gymnasium.

They lift the coffin back on to the trestles.

I'd like to get married. It's the one thing I haven't tried.

HAL. I don't like your living for kicks, baby. Put these neurotic ideas out of your mind and concentrate on the problems of everyday life. We must get the corpse buried before tonight. Be in a tricky position else. And another stretch will be death to my ambitions. I put my not getting on in life down to them persistently sending me to Borstal. I might go permanently bent if this falls through. It's not a pleasant prospect, is it?

The coffin is back upon the trestles.
DENNIS *takes the chewing-gum from his mouth and sticks it under the coffin. He puts on his hat.* HAL *sits.*

Was it Truscott searched your house?

DENNIS. Yes. And he had me down the station for questioning. Gave me a rabbit punch. No, I'm a liar. A rabbit-type punch. Winded me. Took me by the cobblers. Oh, 'strewth, it made me bad.

HAL. Yes, he has a nice line in corporal punishment. Last time he was here he kicked my old lady's cat and he smiled while he did it. How did he get into your house?

DENNIS. He said he was from the sanitary people. My dad let him in. 'Course, I recognized him at once.

HAL. Did you tell him?

DENNIS. Yes.

HAL. What did he say?

DENNIS. Nothing. He kept on about testing the water supply. I asked him if he had a warrant. He said the water board didn't issue warrants.

HAL. You should've phoned the police. Asked for protection.

DENNIS. I did.

HAL. What did they say?

DENNIS. They said that one of their men called Truscott was at our house and why didn't we complain to him?

HAL. What did Truscott say?

DENNIS. He said he was from the water board. My nerves were in shreds by the end of it.

FAY *approaches the door left. Her shadow is cast on the glass panel.*

FAY (*off*). What are you doing, Harold?

HAL *goes to the coffin and kneels in prayer.*

HAL. That brothel I mentioned has swing doors. (*He bows his head.*) You don't often see that, do you?

DENNIS *takes the chair from under the door handle and opens the door quietly.*

DENNIS. We're ready now.

FAY *enters in mourning with a veil over her hair. She carries an embroidered text. Her dress is unzipped at the back. She goes to the wardrobe and tries to open the door. She sees in the mirror that her dress is unzipped, comes to the coffin and bows her head over it.* HAL, *still kneeling, zips her dress up.* MCLEAVY *enters blowing his nose, a sorrowful expression upon his face.*

MCLEAVY (*to* DENNIS). Forgive me being so overwrought, but it's my first bereavement.

DENNIS. The exit of a loved one is always a painful experience.

FAY, *the dress zipped, straightens up.*

FAY. Here – (*she puts the embroidered text on to the coffin.*) – the Ten Commandments. She was a great believer in some of them.

HAL *and* DENNIS *lift the coffin.*

MCLEAVY (*greatly moved, placing a hand on the coffin*). Goodbye, old girl. You've had a lot of suffering. I shall miss you.

HAL *and* DENNIS *go out with the coffin.* FAY *throws back her veil.*

FAY. She's gone. I could feel her presence leaving us. Funny how you know, isn't it?

MCLEAVY. That dress is attractive. Suits you. Black.

FAY. It's another piece of your late wife's finery. Some people would censure me for wearing it. (*She puts a hand on his arm, smiles.*) Are you feeling calmer now?

MCLEAVY. Yes. I've a resilient nature, but death upsets me. I'd rather witness a birth than a death any day. Though the risks involved are greater.

TRUSCOTT *enters left.*

TRUSCOTT. Good afternoon.

FAY. Good afternoon. Who are you?

TRUSCOTT. I am attached to the metropolitan water board. I'm on a fact-finding tour of the area. I'd like to inspect your mains supply.

MCLEAVY. It's outside.

TRUSCOTT. Is it?

Pause, ruminates.

I wonder how it came to be put out there. Most ingenious. You're sure there isn't a tap in this cupboard?

He tries the wardrobe door and smiles.

MCLEAVY. It's in the garden.

TRUSCOTT. Where?

MCLEAVY. I don't know.

TRUSCOTT. I suggest, then, that you find it, sir. Any property belonging to the council must be available on demand. The law is clear on that point.

MCLEAVY. I'll find it at once, sir. I wouldn't wish to place myself outside the law.

He goes off right.

TRUSCOTT (*turning to* FAY). Who has the key to this cupboard?

FAY. The son of the house.

TRUSCOTT. Would he be willing to open it? I'd make it worth his while.

FAY. I've already asked for it to be opened. He refused point-blank.

TRUSCOTT. I see. (*Chews his lip.*) Most significant. You'll be out of the house for some considerable time this afternoon?

FAY. Yes. I'm attending the funeral of my late employer.

TRUSCOTT. Thank you, miss. You've been a great help. (*He smiles, goes to window.*) Who sent the large wreath that has been chosen to decorate the motor?

FAY. The licensee of the King of Denmark. I don't think a publican's tribute should be given pride of place.

TRUSCOTT. You wouldn't, miss. You had a strict upbringing.

FAY. How do you know?

TRUSCOTT. You have a crucifix.

FAY'S *hand goes to the crucifix on her breast.*

It has a dent to one side and engraved on the back the

words: 'St Mary's Convent. Gentiles Only.' It's not difficult to guess at your background from such tell-tale clues.

FAY. You're quite correct. It was a prize for good conduct. The dent was an accident.

TRUSCOTT. Your first husband damaged it.

FAY. During a quarrel.

TRUSCOTT. At the end of which you shot him.

FAY (*taken aback*). You must have access to private information.

TRUSCOTT. Not at all. Guesswork mostly. I won't bore you with the details. The incident happened at the Hermitage Private Hotel. Right?

FAY (*a little alarmed*). This is uncanny.

TRUSCOTT. My methods of deduction can be learned by any-one with a keen eye and a quick brain. When I shook your hand I felt a roughness on one of your wedding rings. A roughness I associate with powder burns and salt. The two together spell a gun and sea air. When found on a wedding ring only one solution is possible.

FAY. How did you know it happened at the Hermitage Private Hotel?

TRUSCOTT. That particular hotel is notorious for tragedies of this kind. I took a chance which paid off.

He takes out his pipe and chews on it.

Has it never occurred to you to wonder why all your hus-bands met with violent deaths?

FAY. They didn't!

TRUSCOTT. Your first was shot. Your second collapsed whilst celebrating the anniversary of the Battle of Mons. Your third fell from a moving vehicle. Your fourth took an over-dose on the eve of his retirement from Sadler's Wells. Your fifth and sixth husbands disappeared. Presumed dead. Your last partner suffered a seizure three nights after marrying you. From what cause?

FAY (*coldly*). I refuse to discuss my private life with you.

TRUSCOTT. For ten years death has been persistently associated with your name.

FAY. You could say the same of an even moderately successful undertaker.

TRUSCOTT. Undertakers have to mix with the dead. It's their duty. You have not that excuse. Seven husbands in less than a decade. There's something seriously wrong with your approach to marriage. I find it frightening that, undeterred by past experience, you're contemplating an eighth engagement.

FAY. How do you know?

TRUSCOTT. You wear another woman's dress as though you were born to it.

FAY (*wide-eyed with wonder*). You amaze me. This dress did belong to Mrs McLeavy.

TRUSCOTT. Elementary detection. The zip is of a type worn by elderly women.

FAY. You should be a detective.

TRUSCOTT. I'm often mistaken for one. Most embarrassing. My wife is frequently pestered by people who are under the impression that she is a policeman's wife. She upbraids me for getting her into such scrapes. (*He laughs.*) You recognize the daily bread of married life, I'm sure. (*He chews on his pipe for a moment.*) When do you intend to propose to Mr McLeavy?

FAY. At once. Delay would be fatal.

TRUSCOTT. Anything taken in combination with yourself usually results in death.

FAY. How dare you speak to me like this! Who are you?

TRUSCOTT *takes out his notebook and pencil.*

TRUSCOTT (*pleasantly*). I'm a council employee who has let his imagination wander. Please forgive me if I've upset you.

He tears a page from the notebook and hands it to FAY.

Sign this chit.

FAY (*looking at it*). It's blank.

TRUSCOTT. That's quite in order. I want you to help me blindly without asking questions.

FAY. I can't sign a blank sheet of paper. Someone might forge my name on a cheque.

TRUSCOTT. Sign my name, then.

FAY. I don't know your name.

TRUSCOTT. Good gracious, what a suspicious mind you have. Sign yourself Queen Victoria. No one would tamper with her account.

FAY *signs the paper and gives it back to* TRUSCOTT.

I think that's all I want from you, miss.

FAY. Will you do one thing for me?

TRUSCOTT. What?

FAY. Let me see you without your hat.

TRUSCOTT (*alarmed*). No. I couldn't possibly. I never take my hat off in front of a lady. It would be discourteous.

MCLEAVY *enters right.*

Have you been successful in your search, sir?

MCLEAVY. Yes. Next to my greenhouse you'll find an iron plaque. Under it is a tap.

TRUSCOTT. Thank you, sir. I shall mention your co-operation in my next report. (*He touches his hat.*) Good afternoon.

He goes off right.

MCLEAVY. I hope he finds what he's looking for. I like to be of assistance to authority.

FAY. We must watch that he doesn't abuse his trust. He showed no credentials.

MCLEAVY. Oh, we can rely on public servants to behave themselves. We must give this man every opportunity to do his
duty. As a good citizen I ignore the stories which bring
officialdom into disrepute.

HAL *enters left.*

HAL. There's a delay in starting the car. A flat tyre. (*Taking
off his coat.*) We're changing the wheel.
MCLEAVY. I hardly think it proper for a mourner to mend the
puncture. Is your mother safe?
HAL. Dennis is guarding the coffin.
MCLEAVY. Be as quick as you can. Your mother hated to miss
an appointment.
HAL. The contents of that coffin are very precious to me. I'm
determined to see they get to the graveyard without mishap.

He goes off left.

MCLEAVY (*with a smile, shaking his head*). It's unusual for him
to show affection. I'm touched by it.
FAY. Mrs McLeavy was a good mother. She has a right to
respect.
MCLEAVY. Yes. I've ordered four hundred rose trees to help
keep her memory green. On a site, only a stone's throw from
the church, I intend to found the 'Mrs Mary McLeavy
Memorial Rose Garden'. It will put Paradise to shame.
FAY. Have you ever seen Paradise?
MCLEAVY. Only in photographs.
FAY. Who took them?
MCLEAVY. Father Jellicoe. He's a widely travelled man.
FAY. You mustn't run yourself into debt.
MCLEAVY. Oh, Mrs McLeavy will pay for the memorial her-
self. The will is as good as proven.

FAY *sits beside him, takes his hand.*

FAY. I don't know whether you can be trusted with a secret, but it would be wrong of me to keep you in the dark a moment longer. Your wife changed her will shortly before she died. She left all her money to me.

MCLEAVY. What! (*Almost fainting.*) Is it legal?

FAY. Perfectly.

MCLEAVY. She must've been drunk. What about me and the boy?

FAY. I'm surprised at you taking this attitude. Have you no sense of decency?

MCLEAVY. Oh, it's God's judgement on me for marrying a Protestant. How much has she left you?

FAY. Nineteen thousand pounds including her bonds and her jewels.

MCLEAVY. Her jewels as well?

FAY. Except her diamond ring. It's too large and unfashionable for a woman to wear. She's left that to Harold.

MCLEAVY. Employing you has cost me a fortune. You must be the most expensive nurse in history.

FAY. You don't imagine that I want the money for myself, do you.

MCLEAVY. Yes.

FAY. That's unworthy of you. I'm most embarrassed by Mrs McLeavy's generosity.

MCLEAVY. You'll destroy the will?

FAY. I wish I could.

MCLEAVY. Why can't you?

FAY. It's a legal document. I could be sued.

MCLEAVY. By whom?

FAY. The beneficiary.

MCLEAVY. That's you. You'd never sue yourself.

FAY. I might. If I was pushed too far. We must find some way of conveying the money into your bank account.

MCLEAVY. Couldn't you just give it to me?

FAY. Think of the scandal.

MCLEAVY. What do you suggest then?

FAY. We must have a joint bank account.

MCLEAVY. Wouldn't that cause an even bigger scandal?

FAY. Not if we were married.

MCLEAVY. Married? But then you'd have my money as well as Mrs McLeavy's.

FAY. That is one way of looking at it.

MCLEAVY. No. I'm too old. My health wouldn't stand up to a young wife.

FAY. I'm a qualified nurse.

MCLEAVY. You'd have to give up your career.

FAY. I'd do it for you.

MCLEAVY. I can give you nothing in return.

FAY. I ask for nothing. I'm a woman. Only half the human race can say that without fear of contradiction. (*She kisses him.*) Go ahead. Ask me to marry you. I've no intention of refusing. On your knees. I'm a great believer in traditional positions.

MCLEAVY. The pains in my legs.

FAY. Exercise is good for them. (MCLEAVY *kneels.*) Use any form of proposal you like. Try to avoid abstract nouns.

HAL *enters left.*

HAL. We're ready. The leader of the Mother's Union has given the signal for tears. (*He picks up his coat.*) We must ride the tide of emotion while it lasts.

FAY. They'll have to wait. Your father is about to propose to me. I think you may stay.

MCLEAVY (*struggling to his feet*). I'm giving no exhibition. Not in front of my son.

HAL. I'm surprised he should wish to marry again. He couldn't do justice to his last wife.

Car horn. DENNIS *enters left.*

DENNIS. Would everybody like to get into the car? We'll have the priest effing and blinding if we're late.

MCLEAVY (*to* FAY). This is so undignified. My wife isn't in her grave.

FAY. And she never will be if you insist on prolonging the proceedings beyond their natural length.

MCLEAVY. I'll propose to you on the way to the cemetery, Nurse McMahon. Will that satisfy you?

DENNIS (*to* FAY). You can't marry him. You know the way I feel about you.

FAY. I couldn't marry you. You're not a Catholic.

DENNIS. You could convert me.

FAY. I'm not prepared to be both wife and missionary.

HAL (*putting an arm round* DENNIS). He's richer than my dad, you know.

FAY. Has he his bank statement on him?

DENNIS. I came out without it.

Car horn.

MCLEAVY. Mrs McLeavy is keeping her Maker waiting. I'll pay my addresses to you after the interment.

Prolonged car horn.

Come on! We'll have a damaged motor horn to pay for next!

FAY. I've decided not to attend. I shall wave. Show my respects from afar.

MCLEAVY. The number of people staying away from the poor woman's funeral is heartbreaking. And I hired a de luxe model car because they're roomier. I could've saved myself the expense.

He goes off left.

DENNIS (*to* FAY). I'd slave for you.

FAY (*pulling on her gloves*). I can't marry boys.

HAL. He'd grow a moustache.

FAY. It really doesn't concern me what he grows. Grow two if it pleases him.

HAL. Would it please you? That's the point.

FAY. The income from fairgrounds might interest me. Otherwise a man with two has no more fascination than a man with one.

DENNIS. A fully productive life isn't possible with a man of Mr McLeavy's age.

FAY. We shall prove you wrong. He'll start a second family under my guidance.

HAL. You're wasting your time. He couldn't propagate a row of tomatoes.

Car horn.

FAY (*to* DENNIS). Get in the car! I've no intention of marrying you.

DENNIS (*to* HAL, *in tears*). She's turned me down. She's broken my heart.

HAL. She doesn't know what she's missing, baby.

DENNIS. But she does! That's what's so humiliating. (*He wipes his eyes with the back of his hand.*) Well, the funeral is off as far as I'm concerned.

HAL. You're driving the car. People will notice your absence.

FAY *is at the wardrobe.*

FAY (*pause*). Where did you get your money?

DENNIS. My auntie left it to me.

FAY. Is that true, Harold?

HAL (*after an inner struggle*). No.

DENNIS. I mean my uncle.

FAY (*to* HAL). Is that true?

HAL (*desperate, looking at* DENNIS). No.

DENNIS. You make our life together impossible. Lie, can't you?

HAL. I can't, baby. It's my upbringing.

Car horn.

DENNIS. Try to control yourself. If I come back and find
you've been telling the truth all afternoon – we're through!

He goes off left. FAY *takes two black-edged handkerchiefs
from her handbag, shakes them out, gives one to* HAL.

FAY. Blow your nose. People expect it.

*She lowers her veil. They both go to the window. They wave.
Sound of a car receding. Pause.* FAY *turns from the window.
She goes to the wardrobe. She throws off her veil.*

Come here. Open this cupboard.

HAL *puts his handkerchief into his pocket.*

Don't hesitate to obey me. Open this cupboard.

HAL. Why are you so interested?

FAY. I've a coatee in there.

HAL. Really?

FAY. I bought it three days ago. I must change. Mourning
gets so grubby if you hang around in it for long.

She looks at HAL *in silence.*

I've got a key. I could see in. Quite easy.

HAL. I've got something in there.

FAY. What?

HAL. A corpse.

FAY. You've added murder to the list of insults heaped upon
your family?

HAL. One doesn't have to murder to acquire a corpse.

FAY. You're running a private mortuary, then?

Pause.

Where are you concealing the money?

HAL. In my mother's coffin.

FAY. That'd be an unusual hiding-place.

Pause.

Where is it now? Answer at once. I shan't repeat my question.

HAL. The money is putting on incorruption. The flesh is still waiting.

FAY. Where is it waiting?

HAL. In that cupboard.

FAY. Open it.

HAL. You have a key.

FAY. I haven't.

HAL. You were lying?

FAY. Yes.

HAL *gives her the key. She opens the wardrobe, looks in, closes the door and screams.*

This is unforgivable. I shall speak to your father.

Pause.

She's standing on her head.

HAL. I concealed nothing from you.

FAY. Your explanation had the ring of truth. Naturally I disbelieved every word.

HAL. I want her buried. Are you prepared to help me?

FAY. Oh, no! I couldn't. This is a case for the authorities.

HAL. You'll never make it to the altar without my help.

FAY. I need no help from you to get a man to bed.

HAL. My father holds it as a cherished belief that a whore is no fit companion for a man.

FAY. As a creed it has more to offer than most.

HAL. My mate Dennis has done you. He speaks of it with relish.

FAY. Young men pepper their conversation with tales of rape. It creates a good impression.

HAL. You never had the blessing of a rape. I was with him at his only ravishment. A bird called Pauline Ching. Broke a tooth in the struggle, she did. It was legal with you. While Jesus pointed to his Sacred Heart, you pointed to yours.

FAY. I never point. It's rude.

HAL. If I tell my father, he'll never marry you.

FAY. I haven't decided whether I wish to marry your father. Your friend is a more interesting proposition.

HAL. He won't be if you grass to the police.

FAY (*pause*). Blackmail? So early in the game.

> HAL *takes out a comb and goes to the mirror. He combs his hair.*

HAL. I want the body stripped. All I ask is an hour or two of Burke and Hare. It isn't a thing someone of the opposite sex can do. And I'm a relative, which complicates the issue.

FAY. You intend a country burial?

HAL. Yes.

FAY. Suppose a dog were to discover her? When they were out hunting for foxes. Do you set no store by the average foxhound?

HAL. Perfectly preserved body of a woman. No sign of foul play. The uniform we'll burn. The underwear you can keep.

FAY. Your mother's underclothes?

HAL. All good stuff.

FAY. I couldn't. Our sizes vary.

HAL. For the bonfire then. Her teeth can go in the river.

FAY. We're nowhere near the river.

HAL. We can borrow your car.

FAY. Provided you pay for the petrol.

HAL. Right.

FAY. Where will she be?

HAL. In the back seat. (*He puts the comb away.*) She always was a back-seat driver.

He opens the wardrobe and wheels the bed to the wardrobe door.

FAY. What about payment?
HAL. Twenty per cent.
FAY. Thirty-three and a third.
HAL. You can keep her wedding ring.
FAY. Is it valuable?
HAL. Very.
FAY. I'll add it to my collection. I already have seven by right of conquest.

   HAL *pulls the screen round the bed.*

Thirty-three and a third and the wedding ring.
HAL. Twenty per cent, the wedding ring and I pay for the petrol?
FAY. Thirty-three and a third, the wedding ring and you pay for the petrol.
HAL. You drive a hard bargain.
FAY. I never bargain.
HAL. Done.

   He throws the mattress cover to her.

Put her in that.

   FAY *goes behind the screen.*

FAY. I need help to get her out of the cupboard.

   HAL *goes behind the screen.*

I'm not taking the head end.
HAL. She won't bite. You have your gloves on.

   They lift the corpse from the wardrobe and lay it on the bed. Something drops from it and rolls away.

FAY. What's that?

HAL (*appearing from behind the screen, searching*). Nothing, nothing.

FAY (*poking her head over the screen*). A screw from the coffin, perhaps?

HAL. Was it the wedding ring?

FAY (*looking*). No. Nothing important.

HAL. I'm inclined to agree.

> FAY *goes behind the screen.* HAL *takes a sheet from off the screen and spreads it on the floor.*

FAY (*from behind the screen*). Lovely-shaped feet your mother had. For a woman of her age.

> *She hands a pair of shoes across the screen.* HAL *places them in the centre of the sheet.*

What will you do with the money?

> *She hands a pair of stockings over the screen.*

HAL. I'd like to run a brothel. (*He pushes the stockings into the shoes.*) I'd run a two-star brothel. And if I prospered I'd graduate to a three-star brothel. I'd advertise 'By Appointment'. Like jam.

> FAY *hands a* W.V.S. *uniform across the screen.* HAL *folds it up and puts it into the sheet.*

I'd have a spade bird. I don't agree with the colour bar. And a Finnish bird. I'd make them kip together. To bring out the contrast.

> FAY *hands a slip across the screen.* HAL *puts it into the pile.*

I'd have two Irish birds. A decent Catholic. And a Protestant. I'd make the Protestant take Catholics. And the Catholic take Protestants. Teach them how the other half lives. I'd have a blonde bird who'd dyed her hair dark. And a dark bird who'd dyed her hair blonde. I'd have a midget. And a tall bird with big tits.

FAY *hands across the screen in quick succession, a pair of corsets, a brassiere and a pair of knickers.* HAL *puts them into the pile.*

FAY. Are you committed to having her teeth removed?
HAL. Yes.

Pause.

I'd have a French bird, a Dutch bird, a Belgian bird, an Italian bird—

FAY *hands a pair of false teeth across the screen.*

—and a bird that spoke fluent Spanish and performed the dances of her native country to perfection. (*He clicks the teeth like castanets.*) I'd call it the Consummatum Est. And it'd be the most famous house of ill-fame in the whole of England.

FAY *appears from behind the screen.* HAL *holds up the teeth.*

These are good teeth. Are they the National Health?
FAY. No. She bought them out of her winnings. She had some good evenings at the table last year.

FAY *folds up the screen. The corpse is lying on the bed, wrapped in the mattress cover, tied with bandages.*

HAL (*approaching the bed, bowing his head*). She was a great lady. Nothing was too good for her. Which is why she had to go.
FAY (*taking a key from her handbag, gives it to* HAL). Fetch the car. Pay cash. It's not to be charged to my account.

TRUSCOTT *approaches the door left. His shadow is cast upon the glass panel. He knocks on the door.* HAL *picks up the sheet with the clothes in it. He looks for somewhere to put them.* FAY *opens the door.* TRUSCOTT *stands outside, smiling.*

TRUSCOTT (*touching his hat*). I'm back again, miss.

> FAY *slams the door.* HAL *stuffs the sheet and clothes into the bedpan attached to the invalid chair.* FAY *pulls the screen round the bed.*

(*Calling.*) Might I have a word with you.

> HAL *closes the lid of the bedpan, concealing the clothes.*

FAY (*calling, answering* TRUSCOTT). Yes.

TRUSCOTT. Let me in, then, I can't hold a conversation through a keyhole. I'm a council employee. I might lose my pension.

> HAL *sits in the invalid chair.* FAY *opens the door.* TRUSCOTT *enters.*

What's going on in this house?

HAL. Nothing.

TRUSCOTT. You admit it? You must be very sure of yourself. Why aren't you both at the funeral? I thought you were mourners.

FAY. We decided not to go. We were afraid we might break down.

TRUSCOTT. That's a selfish attitude to take. The dead can't bury themselves, you know.

> *He takes his pipe from his pocket and plugs it with tobacco.*

FAY. What are you doing here?

TRUSCOTT (*smiling*). I've been having a look round your charming house. Poking and prying.

HAL. Have you a search warrant?

TRUSCOTT. What for?

HAL. To search the house.

TRUSCOTT. But I've already searched the house. I don't want to do it again.

FAY. It's common knowledge what police procedure is. They must have a search warrant.

TRUSCOTT. I'm sure the police must, but as I've already informed you, I am from the water board. And our procedure is different.

He puts the pipe into his mouth, lights it, draws on it.

(*Chewing on his pipe.*) Now, I was sent on a fool's errand a few minutes ago. Unless I'm much mistaken, the object of my search is in that cupboard.

Pause.

Open it for me.

HAL. It isn't locked.

TRUSCOTT. I can't take your word for it, lad.

HAL *opens the wardrobe door.* TRUSCOTT *puts on a pair of spectacles, and stares in. He shakes his head. He takes off his spectacles.*

This puts an entirely different complexion on the matter.

FAY. It's empty.

TRUSCOTT. Exactly. There's still a lot of routine work to be done, I can see that. Would you mind waiting outside, miss? I'd like a word with this lad alone. I'll let you know when you're wanted.

FAY *and* HAL *exchange bewildered glances.* FAY *goes off left.*

(*Laughing pleasantly.*) I always have difficulties with the ladies. They can't accept a *fait accompli*.

Pause. He takes the pipe from his mouth and stares speculatively at HAL.

What do you know of a lad called Dennis?

HAL. He's a mate of mine.

TRUSCOTT. You don't want to spend your time with a youth like him. He's not your type. He's got five pregnancies to his credit.

HAL. Anyone can make a mistake.

TRUSCOTT. Maybe. But he's obviously getting into the habit of making mistakes. Where does he engender these unwanted children? There are no open spaces. The police patrol regularly. It should be next to impossible to commit the smallest act of indecency, let alone beget a child. Where does he do it?

HAL. On crowded dance floors during the rhumba.

FAY *enters left.*

TRUSCOTT (*removing his pipe, patiently*). I'm a busy man, miss. Do as you're told and wait outside.

FAY. What's your name?

TRUSCOTT. I prefer to remain anonymous for the present.

FAY. Your Christian name.

TRUSCOTT. I'm not a practising Christian.

FAY. Is it Jim?

TRUSCOTT. No.

FAY. A man at the door says it is.

TRUSCOTT. I'd like to help him, but I'm not prepared to admit to any name other than my own.

FAY. He says his name is Meadows.

TRUSCOTT (*pause, nods his head sagely*). One of my names is Jim. Clearly this fellow is in possession of the fact and wishes to air his knowledge. I shall speak to him.

TRUSCOTT *goes off left.*

FAY (*closing the door, whispers*). There's a uniformed police-man at the door! They're on to us.

HAL. It's bluff.

FAY. No. God works for them. They have Him in their pockets like we've always been taught.

HAL. We've got to get rid of him. He'll find the body next.

He opens the wardrobe door and puts FAY'S *shoes and the coathanger inside. He closes the door quickly and turns to* FAY.

Remember when we were wrapping her up?

FAY. It's not something I care to reminisce about.

HAL. Something dropped out? We couldn't find it?

FAY. Yes.

HAL. I know what it was.

FAY. What?

HAL. One of her eyes!

They drop to their knees. They search. TRUSCOTT *enters. They stand.*

TRUSCOTT (*smiling*). Just a bobby making a nuisance of himself.

He goes to the screen and glances behind it. Pause. He takes the pipe from his mouth.

The theft of a Pharaoh is something which hadn't crossed my mind.

He folds the screen revealing the corpse, swathed in the mattress cover and tied with bandages.

Whose mummy is this?

HAL. Mine.

TRUSCOTT. Whose was it before?

HAL. I'm an only child.

TRUSCOTT. A word of warning. Don't take the mickey. You'll make me angry. (*He smiles.*) O.K.?

FAY. It's not a mummy. It's a dummy. I used to sew my dresses on it.

TRUSCOTT. What sex is it?

FAY. I call it 'she' because of my sewing. The garments were female and because I'm literal-minded I chose to believe I was making them on a lady.

TRUSCOTT. Splendid. Excellently put.

HAL. No actual evidence of sex can be given. It's contrary to English law.

TRUSCOTT. Yes, a tailor's dummy provided with evidence of sex would fill the mind of the average magistrate with misgiving. Why is it wrapped?

HAL. We were taking it in the car.

FAY. To a carnival. She's part of a display.

TRUSCOTT. What part?

FAY. A sewing-class. Prewar. The difference in technique is to be demonstrated.

TRUSCOTT. Is this dummy a frequent visitor to exhibitions?

FAY. Yes.

TRUSCOTT. When is the object's outing to take place?

FAY. It isn't going now.

TRUSCOTT. The treat has been cancelled?

FAY. Yes.

TRUSCOTT. Why?

HAL. My mate Dennis was to have arranged transport. He let us down.

TRUSCOTT. I can believe that. From all I've heard of your friend I'd say he was quite capable of disappointing a tailor's dummy.

He puts his pipe into the corner of his mouth. He takes out his notebook and makes notes.

You claim this object is awaiting transport to a carnival where it will be used to demonstrate the continuity of British needlework?

FAY. Yes.

TRUSCOTT. Sounds a reasonable explanation. Quite reasonable.

He puts the notebook away and chews on his pipe. He observes HAL narrowly.

What were you doing on Saturday night?

Pause as HAL tries to avoid telling the truth. He stares at FAY in an agony.

HAL (*at last*). I was in bed.

> FAY *breathes a sigh of relief.*

TRUSCOTT. Can you confirm that, miss?

FAY. Certainly not.

TRUSCOTT (*to* HAL). What were you doing in bed?

HAL. Sleeping.

TRUSCOTT. Do you seriously expect me to believe that? A man of your age behaving like a child? What was your mate doing on Saturday night?

HAL. He was in bed as well.

TRUSCOTT. You'll tell me next he was sleeping.

HAL. I expect he was.

TRUSCOTT (*to* FAY). What a coincidence, miss. Don't you agree? Two young men who know each other very well, spend their nights in separate beds. Asleep. It sounds highly unlikely to me. (*To* HAL.) What is your excuse for knowing him?

HAL. He's clever. I'm stupid, see.

TRUSCOTT. Why do you make such stupid remarks?

HAL. I'm a stupid person. That's what I'm trying to say.

TRUSCOTT. What proof have I that you're stupid. Give me an example of your stupidity.

HAL. I can't.

TRUSCOTT. Why not? I don't believe you're stupid at all.

HAL. I am. I had a hand in the bank job.

> FAY *draws a sharp breath.* HAL *sits frozen.* TRUSCOTT *takes his pipe from his mouth.*

(*With a nervous laugh.*) There, that's stupid, isn't it? Telling you that.

TRUSCOTT (*also laughing*). You must be stupid if you expect me to believe you. Why, if you had a hand in the bank job, you wouldn't tell me.

FAY. Not unless he was stupid.

TRUSCOTT. But he is stupid. He's just admitted it. He must be
the stupidest criminal in England. Unless – (*He regards* HAL
with mounting suspicion.) – unless he's the cleverest. What
was your motive in confessing to the bank job?

HAL. To prove I'm stupid.

TRUSCOTT. But you've proved the opposite.

HAL. Yes.

TRUSCOTT (*baffled, gnawing his lip*). There's more to this than
meets the eye. I'm tempted to believe that you did have a
hand in the bank job. Yes. I shall inform my superior officer.
He will take whatever steps he thinks fit. I may be required
to make an arrest.

FAY. The water board can't arrest people.

TRUSCOTT. They can in certain circumstances.

FAY. What circumstances?

TRUSCOTT. I'm not prepared to reveal the inner secrets of the
water board to a member of the general public. (*To* HAL.)
Where's the money?

HAL (*closing his eyes, taking a deep breath*). It's being buried.

TRUSCOTT. Who's burying it?

HAL. Father Jellicoe, S.J.

TRUSCOTT. Come here! Come here!

    HAL *goes over, his hands trembling as they button up his coat.*

I'm going to ask you a question or two. I want sensible
answers. None of your piss-taking. Is that understood? Do I
make myself plain? I'm talking English. Do you understand?

HAL. Yes.

TRUSCOTT. All right then. As long as we know.

    A pause, in which he studies HAL.

Now, be sensible. Where's the money?

    HAL *looks at his watch.*

HAL. By now I'd say it was half-way up the aisle of the Church of St Barnabas and St Jude.

He half turns away. TRUSCOTT *brings his fist down on the back of* HAL'S *neck.* HAL *cries out in pain and collapses on to the floor rubbing his shoulder.*

FAY (*indignant*). How dare you! He's only a boy.

TRUSCOTT. I'm not impressed by his sex, miss. (*To* HAL.) I asked for the truth.

HAL. I'm telling the truth.

TRUSCOTT. Understand this, lad. You can't get away with cheek. Kids nowadays treat any kind of authority as a challenge. We'll challenge you. If you oppose me in my duty, I'll kick those teeth through the back of your head. Is that clear?

HAL. Yes.

Door chimes.

FAY. Would you excuse me, Inspector?

TRUSCOTT (*wiping his brow*). You're at liberty to answer your own doorbell, miss. That is how we tell whether or not we live in a free country.

FAY *goes off left.*

(*Standing over* HAL.) Where's the money?

HAL. In church.

TRUSCOTT *kicks* HAL *violently.* HAL *cries out in terror and pain.*

TRUSCOTT. Don't lie to me!

HAL. I'm not lying! It's in church!

TRUSCOTT (*shouting, knocking* HAL *to the floor*). Under any other political system I'd have you on the floor in tears!

HAL (*crying*). You've got me on the floor in tears.

TRUSCOTT. Where's the money?

HAL. I've told you. In church. They're quoting St Paul over it.

TRUSCOTT. I don't care if they're quoting the Highway Code over it. One more chance. Where is it?

HAL (*desperate, trying to protect himself*). In church! In church! My dad's watching the last rites of a hundred and four thousand quid!

> TRUSCOTT *jerks* HAL *from the floor, beating and kicking and punching him.* HAL *screams with pain.*

TRUSCOTT. I'll hose you down! I'll chlorinate you!

> HAL *tries to defend himself, his nose is bleeding.*

You'll be laughing on the other side of your bloody face.

> FAY *enters left, supporting* MCLEAVY, *who is heavily bandaged.*

FAY. They've had an accident!

> TRUSCOTT *leaves* HAL, *pulls the bed from the wall and shoves it to* MCLEAVY, *who faints on to it, just missing the corpse.* HAL *drags the corpse from the bed and shoves it behind the screen.*

TRUSCOTT (*to* MCLEAVY). Have you reported the accident?

> MCLEAVY *opens his mouth. He is too overcome by emotion to speak.*

FAY. It's the shock. Taken away his power of speech, it has.

TRUSCOTT. Has this happened before?

FAY. Yes. Six or seven times.

TRUSCOTT. If he's going to make a habit of it he ought to learn a sign language. (*To* MCLEAVY.) Do you understand me, sir?

> MCLEAVY *closes his eyes, shudders.* TRUSCOTT *straightens up.*

I've known people communicate with the dead in half this time.

MCLEAVY (*moaning*). Oh . . . Oh . . .

TRUSCOTT. What has happened, sir?

MCLEAVY. I've had an accident.

TRUSCOTT. I shall have to make a full report.

He takes out his note-book.

MCLEAVY. Are you qualified?

TRUSCOTT. That needn't concern you at present, sir. I shall let you know later. Now give me a full statement.

MCLEAVY *passes a hand across his brow and clears his throat.*

MCLEAVY. We set off in high spirits. The weather was humid, a heat mist covered the sky. The road to the graveyard lay uphill. It was a sad occasion for me. In spite of this I kept a tight hold on my emotions, refusing to show the extent of my loss. Along the route perfect strangers had the courtesy to raise their hats. We got admiring glances for the flowers and sympathetic nods for me.

Pause.

The dignity of the event was unsurpassed.

He bows his head, everyone waits. TRUSCOTT *taps sharply on the bedrail with his pencil.*

Then, as the solemn procession was half-way up the hill, a lorry, clearly out of control, came hurtling down on top of us. It struck the first car, holding the remains, and killed the undertaker—

HAL. Not Dennis!

MCLEAVY. No. Mr Walter Tracey. The hearse was a wreck within seconds. Meanwhile the second part of the cortège crashed into the smoking wreckage. I was flung to one side, hitting my head on the bodywork of the vehicle. The next thing I knew I was being helped out by passers-by. The road looked like a battlefield. Strewn with the injured and dying. Blood, glass.

He chokes. Pause.

Several fires were started.

HAL. Was the actual fabric of the coffin damaged?

MCLEAVY. No. Your mother is quite safe.

HAL. No dents? No holes?

MCLEAVY. No. People remarked on the extreme durability of the lid. I was about to give the undertaker a recommendation. Then I remembered that he wasn't capable of receiving one.

TRUSCOTT. Surely he understood when he took on the job that he couldn't make capital out of his own death?

FAY. Where is the coffin?

MCLEAVY. Outside.

FAY (*to* TRUSCOTT). Can it be brought in?

TRUSCOTT. By all means. We mustn't keep a lady waiting.

HAL *goes off.* TRUSCOTT *turns to* MCLEAVY.

Why are you bandaged? Is that a result of the accident?

MCLEAVY. Indirectly. My wounds stem from a fear-crazed Afghan hound that was being exercised at the time. I was bitten about the face and hands. In my nervous state I was an easy target.

TRUSCOTT. Did you take the owner's name?

MCLEAVY. No.

TRUSCOTT. It all seems highly irregular. The dog will have to be destroyed.

MCLEAVY. I don't hold it responsible for its actions. It was frightened.

TRUSCOTT. I've been frightened myself on occasions. I've never bitten anyone. These people should learn to control their pets.

MCLEAVY. The woman who owned the dog had fainted.

TRUSCOTT. She sounds an unstable kind of person to me.

HAL and DENNIS enter with the coffin. It is charred, blackened and smoking.

FAY. Who'd think she'd be back so soon?

MCLEAVY. She could never make up her mind in life. Death hasn't changed her.

DENNIS. Your wreaths have been blown to buggery, Mr McLeavy. We might manage a repair job on that big harp.

HAL. What are we going to do for the replay?

MCLEAVY. Buy fresh ones, I suppose. Always some new expense.

The coffin is set down. The side falls away, revealing the banknotes inside. DENNIS stands in front of the coffin, shielding the contents from TRUSCOTT and MCLEAVY. MCLEAVY holds out a hand and tries to shake DENNIS'S hand.

(*To* TRUSCOTT.) You must congratulate this boy. He rescued the coffin from the blazing car at considerable personal risk.

TRUSCOTT (*dryly*). If he behaves with such consideration to a dead woman, what might we not expect with a live one?

HAL. We need a finishing touch. Know what it is? A holy image. Centre. Between candles.

FAY. I have a Madonna.

HAL. What could be better? Make a gesture. She knew what disappointment was, didn't she? Same as us. A little imagination. What wonders can't it accomplish.

DENNIS. Oh, yes. We've found in the trade that an impression can be created with quite humble materials: a candle, half a yard of velvet and a bunch of anemones and the effect is of a lying in state.

MCLEAVY. My photo of His Holiness would enhance the scene, only it's three Popes out of date.

FAY. Mrs McLeavy won't mind. She wasn't a woman who followed the fashions. Go and get it.

MCLEAVY *stands, moves to the door.* TRUSCOTT *bars his path.*

TRUSCOTT. I must ask you to remain where you are. No one is to leave without my permission.

MCLEAVY. Why?

TRUSCOTT. When you disobey my orders, sir, you make my job doubly difficult.

MCLEAVY. On what authority do you give orders?

TRUSCOTT. You'd be considerably happier if you allowed me to do my duty without asking questions.

MCLEAVY. Who are you?

TRUSCOTT. I'm an official of the Metropolitan Water Board, sir, as I've already told you.

MCLEAVY. But the water board has no power to keep law-abiding citizens confined to their rooms.

TRUSCOTT. Not if the citizens are law abiding.

MCLEAVY. Whether they're law abiding or not the water board has no power.

TRUSCOTT. I don't propose to argue hypothetical cases with you, sir. Remain where you are till further notice.

MCLEAVY. I shall take legal advice.

TRUSCOTT. That is as may be. I've no power to prevent you.

MCLEAVY. I want to telephone my lawyer.

TRUSCOTT. I can't allow you to do that. It would be contrary to regulations. We've no case against you.

TRUSCOTT *chews on his pipe.* MCLEAVY *stares in fury.*

FAY. Can't he fetch the Pope's photo?

TRUSCOTT. Only if some responsible person accompanies him.

HAL. You're a responsible person. You could accompany him.

TRUSCOTT. What proof have I that I'm a responsible person?

DENNIS. If you weren't responsible you wouldn't be given the power to behave as you do.

TRUSCOTT *removes his pipe, considers.*

TRUSCOTT. That is perfectly correct. In which case I shall accompany you, sir. Come with me.

TRUSCOTT *and* MCLEAVY *go off left.*

HAL (*closing the door*). We must return the remains to the coffin and the money to the cupboard.

DENNIS. Why?

FAY. Mr McLeavy may ask for the coffin to be opened. Formaldehyde and three morticians have increased his wife's allure.

DENNIS. But a corpse is only attractive to another corpse.

HAL. We can't rely on him having heard that.

DENNIS *begins to unscrew the coffin lid.* FAY *and* HAL *drag the corpse from behind the screen.*

DENNIS (*looking up*). What's that!

FAY. Mrs McLeavy.

DENNIS (*to* HAL). How much have you told her?

HAL. Everything.

DENNIS. We've never involved a woman in anything unsavoury before.

He takes the lid off the coffin. FAY *piles money into his arms.* HAL *does the same.*

(*To* FAY.) Half of this money is mine. Will you marry me?

HAL. We're splitting the money three ways now, baby. You'll have thirty-four thousand.

DENNIS (*to* FAY). Is that enough?

FAY. You've a slight lead on Mr McLeavy at the moment.

She kisses him. DENNIS *trembles and drops the money back into the coffin.*

HAL (*angry*). Hurry up! What's the matter with you?

DENNIS. My hands are trembling. It's excitement at the prospect of becoming engaged.

HAL. You're too easily aroused. That's your trouble.

MCLEAVY'S *shadow appears on the glass panel.* DENNIS *tips the money into the coffin.*

MCLEAVY (*off*). I'll complain to my M.P. I'll have you reported.

HAL *shoves the lid on to the coffin.* MCLEAVY *enters.*

He's turned the water off. I've just been trying to use the toilet—

FAY (*standing in front of him, preventing him seeing the corpse*). Oh, please! You don't have to explain.

HAL *tries to drag the corpse away.* DENNIS *opens the wardrobe.*

MCLEAVY. I don't believe he's anything to do with the water board. I was handcuffed out there. D'you know that? Handcuffed.

He sees the corpse. He gives a shriek of horror.

What in Heaven's name is that!

FAY. It's my appliance.

MCLEAVY. I've never seen it before.

FAY. I kept it in my room. It was personal.

MCLEAVY. What is it doing down here?

FAY. I'm going to do some work. For charity.

MCLEAVY. What kind of work?

FAY. I'm making the vestments for Our Lady's festival. I was commissioned. My altar cloth at Easter brought me to the attention of the Committee.

MCLEAVY. My congratulations. You'll want plenty of room to work. (*To* DENNIS.) Take Nurse McMahon's applicance to my study.

FAY (*anxious, with a smile*). It's most kind of you, Mr McLeavy, but I'd prefer to work down here. Mrs McLeavy's presence will bring me inspiration.

MCLEAVY. Very well, you have my permission to work down here. I look forward to seeing the finished results.

TRUSCOTT *enters*.

TRUSCOTT (*To* MCLEAVY). Do you still want your padre's photograph, sir?

MCLEAVY. Yes.

TRUSCOTT. You'll find a policeman outside. He will accompany you. Off you go.

MCLEAVY. I resent your manner of speaking! I'm the householder. I can't be ordered about like this.

TRUSCOTT (*shoving him to the door*). Don't make my job any more tiring than it is, sir. Fetch the photograph in question and wait outside until I call.

MCLEAVY *goes off left*.

(*To* DENNIS.) I want a word with you. (*To* HAL *and* FAY.) The rest of you outside!

HAL. Can't I stay with him? He's the nervous type.

TRUSCOTT. I'm nervous as well. I'll be company for him—

FAY. It'd be better if I was present. He's more relaxed in the company of women.

TRUSCOTT. He'll have to come to terms with his psychological peculiarity. Out you go!

FAY *and* HAL *go off left*.

(TRUSCOTT *faces* DENNIS, *the corpse between them*.) Now then, I'm going to ask a few questions. I want sensible answers. I've had enough fooling about for one day. (*He observes* DENNIS *narrowly*.) Have you ever been in prison?

DENNIS. Yes.

TRUSCOTT. What for?

DENNIS. Stealing overcoats and biting a policeman.

TRUSCOTT. The theft of an article of clothing is excusable. But policemen, like red squirrels, must be protected. You were rightly convicted. What do you know of paternity orders?

DENNIS. Is that when birds say you've put them in the club?

TRUSCOTT. Don't try to evade the issue. How many women have you made pregnant?

DENNIS. Five.

TRUSCOTT. You scatter your seed along the pavements without regard to age or sex. (*He taps the corpse.*) What are you doing with this? Have you taken up sewing?

DENNIS. I was putting it in the cupboard.

TRUSCOTT. Why?

DENNIS. To keep it hidden.

TRUSCOTT. Don't try to pull the wool over my eyes. I've been told the whole pathetic story. You ought to be ashamed of yourself.

DENNIS (*pause, with resignation*). Am I under arrest, then?

TRUSCOTT. I wish you were. Unfortunately what you've done isn't illegal.

DENNIS (*pause, with surprise*). When did they change the law?

TRUSCOTT. There never was any law.

DENNIS. Has it all been a leg-pull? My uncle did two years.

TRUSCOTT. What for?

DENNIS. Armed robbery.

TRUSCOTT. That is against the law.

DENNIS. It used to be.

TRUSCOTT. It still is.

DENNIS. I thought the law had been changed.

TRUSCOTT. Who told you that?

DENNIS. You did.

TRUSCOTT. When?

DENNIS. Just now. I thought there'd been a reappraisal of society's responsibilities towards the criminal.

TRUSCOTT. You talk like a judge.

DENNIS. I've met so many.

TRUSCOTT. I'm not impressed by your fine friends.

He chews on his pipe and watches DENNIS *closely.*

Where's the money from the bank job?

DENNIS. What bank job?

TRUSCOTT. Where's it buried?

DENNIS. Buried?

TRUSCOTT. Your mate says it's been buried.

DENNIS (*indignant*). He's a liar!

TRUSCOTT. A very intelligent reply. You're an honest lad. (*He smiles and puts an arm around* DENNIS'S *shoulders.*) Are you prepared to co-operate with me? I'll see you're all right.

DENNIS *edges away.*

I'll put a good word in for you.

DENNIS (*nervous, laughing to hid his embarrassment*). Can't we stand away from the window? I don't want anybody to see me talking to a policeman.

TRUSCOTT. I'm not a policeman.

DENNIS. Aren't you?

TRUSCOTT. No. I'm from the Metropolitan Water Board.

DENNIS. You're the law! You gave me a kicking down the station.

TRUSCOTT. I don't remember doing so.

DENNIS. Well, it's all in the day's work to you, isn't it?

TRUSCOTT. What were you doing down the station?

DENNIS. I was on sus.

TRUSCOTT. What were you suspected of?

DENNIS. The bank job.

TRUSCOTT. And you complain you were beaten?

DENNIS. Yes.

TRUSCOTT. Did you tell anyone?

DENNIS. Yes.

TRUSCOTT. Who?

DENNIS. The officer in charge.

TRUSCOTT. What did he say?

DENNIS. Nothing.

TRUSCOTT. Why not?

DENNIS. He was out of breath with kicking.

TRUSCOTT. I hope you're prepared to substantiate these accusations, lad. What evidence have you?

DENNIS. My bruises.

TRUSCOTT. What is the official version of those?

DENNIS. Resisting arrest.

TRUSCOTT. I can see nothing unreasonable in that. You want to watch yourself. Making unfounded allegations. You'll find yourself in serious trouble.

He takes DENNIS *by the collar and shakes him.*

If I ever hear you accuse the police of using violence on a prisoner in custody again, I'll take you down to the station and beat the eyes out of your head.

He shoves DENNIS *away.*

Now, get out!

DENNIS *is about to leave the corpse.*

And take that thing with you. I don't want to see it in here again.

DENNIS *goes off left with the corpse.*
TRUSCOTT *closes the door and, as he does so, sees something on the floor. He puts his pipe into the corner of his mouth and picks up the glass eye. He holds it to the light in order to get a better view. Puzzled. He sniffs at it. He holds it close to his ear. He rattles it. He takes out a pocket magnifying-glass and stares hard at it. He gives a brief exclamation of horror and surprise.*

Curtain

Act Two

TRUSCOTT, *by the window, is examining the eye under a pocket magnifying-glass.*

MCLEAVY *enters carrying a photograph of Pope Pius XII.* FAY *follows him.*

MCLEAVY. Is it possible to use the toilet, sir?

TRUSCOTT (*putting the eye into his pocket*). The water is off.

FAY. Who turned it off?

TRUSCOTT. My men did.

MCLEAVY (*handing the photograph to* FAY). I'm getting on the phone. I'll have your particulars filed.

TRUSCOTT. I've disconnected the telephone.

MCLEAVY. Why?

TRUSCOTT. You always begin your sentences with 'Why?' Did they teach you to at school?

MCLEAVY. Now, look here – I've a right to know – are you from the sanitary people? I never knew they had power over the post office. Aren't they separate entities? (*To* FAY.) The water board and the post office? Or have they had a merger? (*To* TRUSCOTT.) They'd never connect up the water board and the post office, would they?

TRUSCOTT. I'm not in a position to say, sir.

MCLEAVY. Produce your warrant and you're justified. If not, get out of my house. Even a Government department should take account of death.

TRUSCOTT. Less of that. I must ask you to respect my cloth.

MCLEAVY (*to* FAY). Is he a priest?

FAY. If he is he's an unfrocked one.

MCLEAVY (*stares at* TRUSCOTT, *goes closer to him, wonderingly*).
Who are you?

TRUSCOTT. My name is Truscott.

MCLEAVY. What in Hell kind of a name is that? Is it an
anagram? You're not bloody human, that's for sure. We're
being made the victims of some kind of interplanetary rag.
(*To* FAY.) He's probably luminous in the dark. (*To* TRUS-
COTT.) Come on, I don't care what infernal power you
represent. I want a straight answer.

TRUSCOTT *regards* MCLEAVY *calmly and in silence.*

I'll go next door – they're Dubliners. If you're the Angel of
the Lord Himself, they'll mix it with you.

TRUSCOTT. I've warned you already about leaving this room.
Do as you're told or take the consequences.

MCLEAVY. I'll take the consequences.

TRUSCOTT. I can't allow you to do that.

MCLEAVY. You've no power to stop me.

TRUSCOTT. I must disagree. I'm acting under orders.

MCLEAVY. Whose?

TRUSCOTT. My superior officer's.

MCLEAVY. I don't believe he exists!

TRUSCOTT. If you don't control yourself, I shall have to
caution you.

MCLEAVY. I know we're living in a country whose respect for
the law is proverbial: who'd give power of arrest to the
traffic lights if three women magistrates and a Liberal M.P.
would only suggest it; but I've never heard of an employee
of the water board nicking a kid for stealing apples, let alone
a grown man for doubting whether he had any right to be
on the planet.

Silence. TRUSCOTT *removes his pipe from his mouth slowly,
weighing his words before he speaks.*

TRUSCOTT. If you'll give me your undivided attention for a few moments, sir, I promise you we'll have this whole case sorted out. It isn't a game we're playing. It's my duty, and I must do it to the best of my ability.

The door right is flung open, DENNIS *and* HAL *burst in with the corpse.* TRUSCOTT *looks steadily and searchingly at them. He points to the corpse with his pipe.*

What are you doing with that thing?

DENNIS. We were taking it outside.

TRUSCOTT. Why? Did it need the air?

HAL. We were putting it in the garage.

TRUSCOTT. This isn't the garage. What do you mean by bringing it back into this room?

HAL. A police sergeant was in the garage.

TRUSCOTT. I'm sure he has no particular aversion to sharing a garage with a tailor's dummy.

HAL. He wanted to undress it.

TRUSCOTT. What possible objection could there be to an officer undressing a dummy?

DENNIS. It isn't decent.

HAL. It's a Catholic.

TRUSCOTT (*with contempt*). The things you say are quite ludicrous, lad. (*He laughs mirthlessly.*) Ho, ho ho. Take it to the garage. The bobby won't interfere with it. He's a married man with children.

No one moves. TRUSCOTT *chews on his pipe; he takes pipe from his mouth.*

Go on! Do as I say.

FAY. No! I'd rather it didn't go. I want it here.

TRUSCOTT. Why?

FAY. It's valuable.

TRUSCOTT. Has its value increased during the last few minutes?

FAY. No.

TRUSCOTT. If it's your usual custom to encourage young men to run up and down garden paths with tailor's dummies, you must be stopped from exercising such arbitrary power.

FAY. I did want it in the garage, but after what has been said I feel I can't allow her out of my sight.

TRUSCOTT. Really, miss, your relationship with that object verges on the criminal. Has no one in this house any normal feelings? I've never come across such people. If there's any more of it, I shall arrest the lot of you.

MCLEAVY. How does the water board go about making an arrest?

TRUSCOTT. You must have realized by now, sir, that I am not from the water board?

MCLEAVY. I have. Your behaviour was causing me grave concern.

TRUSCOTT. Any deception I practised was never intended to deceive you, sir. You are – if I may say so – an intelligent man. (*He laughs to himself.*) You saw through my disguise at once. It was merely a ruse to give me time to review the situation. To get my bearings on a very tricky assignment. Or two tricky assignments. As you will shortly realize. (*He smiles and bows to* MCLEAVY.) You have before you a man who is quite a personage in his way – Truscott of the Yard. Have you never heard of Truscott? The man who tracked down the limbless girl killer? Or was that sensation before your time?

HAL. Who would kill a limbless girl?

TRUSCOTT. She was the killer.

HAL. How did she do it if she was limbless?

TRUSCOTT. I'm not prepared to answer that question to anyone outside the profession. We don't want a carbon-copy murder on our hands. (*To* MCLEAVY.) Do you realize what I'm doing here?

MCLEAVY. No. Your every action has been a mystery to me.

TRUSCOTT. That is as it should be. The process by which the

police arrive at the solution to a mystery is, in itself, a
mystery. We've reason to believe that a number of crimes
have been committed under your roof. There was no legal
excuse for a warrant. We had no proof. However, the water
board doesn't need a warrant to enter private houses. And
so I availed myself of this loophole in the law. It's for your
own good that Authority behaves in this seemingly alarming
way. (*With a smile.*) Does my explanation satisfy you?

MCLEAVY. Oh, yes, Inspector. You've a duty to do. My
personal freedom must be sacrificed. I have no further
questions.

TRUSCOTT. Good. I shall proceed to bring the crimes to light.
Beginning with the least important.

HAL. What is that?

TRUSCOTT. Murder.

FAY (*anxiously*). Murder?

TRUSCOTT. Yes, murder. (*To* MCLEAVY.) Your wife passed
away three days ago? What did she die of?

FAY. The death certificate is perfectly legible.

TRUSCOTT. Reading isn't an occupation we encourage among
police officers. We try to keep the paper work down to a
minimum. (*To* MCLEAVY.) Have you no grumble at the
way your wife died?

MCLEAVY. None.

TRUSCOTT. You're easily satisfied, I see. I am not.

FAY. Mrs McLeavy's doctor signed the death certificate.

TRUSCOTT. So I understand. But he'd just come from diagnos-
ing a most unusual pregnancy. His mind was so occupied by
the nature of the case that he omitted to take all factors into
consideration and signed in a fuzz of scientific disbelief. Has
anyone seen Mrs McLeavy since she died?

HAL. How could we?

TRUSCOTT. Can all of you swear you've had no commerce with
the dead?

DENNIS. We're not mediums.

TRUSCOTT. That's a pity. It would have considerably simplified my task if you had been.

FAY. I wasn't going to mention it, but I had a psychic experience last night. Three parts of Mrs McLeavy materialized to me as I was brushing my hair.

TRUSCOTT. Was her fate discussed?

FAY. Yes. In great detail.

MCLEAVY. I never knew you had visions.

TRUSCOTT (to FAY). Mrs McLeavy and I are perhaps the two people most closely involved in her death. I'd be interested to hear her on the subject.

FAY. She accused her husband of murder.

Sensation.

MCLEAVY. Me? Are you sure she accused me?

FAY. Yes.

MCLEAVY. Complete extinction has done nothing to silence her slanderous tongue.

TRUSCOTT. Was anyone with her at the end? (*To* HAL.) Were you?

HAL. Yes.

TRUSCOTT. Was she uneasy? Did she leave no last message?

HAL. No.

TRUSCOTT. Was this her usual custom?

HAL. She hadn't died before.

TRUSCOTT. Not to the best of your knowledge. Though I've no doubt our information isn't as up to date as we supposed. Did she whisper no last words? As you bent to kiss her cheek before she expired?

HAL. She spoke of a book.

TRUSCOTT. Which?

HAL. A broken binding recurred.

TRUSCOTT. Was it a metaphor?

HAL. I took it to be so.

TRUSCOTT *goes to the bookcase. He takes down a book.*

TRUSCOTT. Apart from Bibles, which are notorious for broken bindings, there is this – The Trial of Phyllis McMahon. Nurse accused of murdering her patient.

He fixes FAY *with a steely look; she turns pale.*

One of my own cases.

He turns over pages, staring hard and with recognition at the photograph.

Look at this photograph.
HAL. It's you.
TRUSCOTT. Yes, most unflattering, isn't it? They always choose the worst. I cannot get them to print a decent picture.

He tears the photograph from the book, screws it into a ball and stuffs it into his pocket.

DENNIS. Is there a photo of the nurse?
TRUSCOTT. Unfortunately not. Someone has torn every picture of the nurse from the book.

Once again he turns his piercing gaze upon FAY; *she looks uncomfortable.*

However, we have something equally damning – the handwriting of the accused.

He opens the book at a page of handwriting.

And here – (*Triumphantly he takes a sheet of paper from his pocket.*) – the evidence on which I propose to convict: a recent specimen of the handwriting of your late wife's nurse. Identical in every respect.
MCLEAVY (*staring at the sheet of paper*). But this is signed Queen Victoria.

TRUSCOTT. One of her many aliases.

MCLEAVY *stares in amazement at the evidence.*

HAL. If it was one of your own cases, how is it she didn't recognize you?

TRUSCOTT. Two very simple reasons. I conduct my cases under an assumed voice and I am a master of disguise. (*He takes off his hat.*) You see – a complete transformation. (*To* MCLEAVY.) You've had a lucky escape, sir. You'd've been the victim of a murder bid inside a month. We've had the tabs on her for years. Thirteen fatal accidents, two cases of suspected fish poisoning. One unexplained disappearance. She's practised her own form of genocide for a decade and called it nursing.

FAY (*staring at him, agitatedly*). I never killed anyone.

TRUSCOTT. At the George V hospital in Holyhead eighty-seven people died within a week. How do you explain that?

FAY. It was the geriatric ward. They were old.

TRUSCOTT. They had a right to live, same as anybody else.

FAY. I was in the children's ward.

TRUSCOTT. How many innocents did you massacre – Phyllis?

FAY. None.

TRUSCOTT. I fail to see why you choose to cloak the episode in mystery. You can't escape.

FAY. Mrs McLeavy accused her husband.

TRUSCOTT. We can't accept the evidence of a ghost. The problems posed would be insuperable.

FAY. You must prove me guilty. That is the law.

TRUSCOTT. You know nothing of the law. I know nothing of the law. That makes us equal in the sight of the law.

FAY. I'm innocent till I'm proved guilty. This is a free country. The law is impartial.

TRUSCOTT. Who's been filling your head with that rubbish?

FAY. I can't be had for anything. You've no proof.

TRUSCOTT. When I make out my report I shall say that you've

given me a confession. It could prejudice your case if I have to forge one.

FAY. I shall deny that I've confessed.

TRUSCOTT. Perjury is a serious crime.

FAY. Have you no respect for the truth?

TRUSCOTT. We have a saying under the blue lamp 'Waste time on the truth and you'll be pounding the beat until the day you retire.'

FAY (*breaking down*). The British police force used to be run by men of integrity.

TRUSCOTT. That is a mistake which has been rectified. Come along now. I can't stand here all day.

FAY (*drying her eyes*). My name is Phyllis Jean McMahon alias Fay Jean McMahon. I am twenty-eight years of age and a nurse by profession. On the third of December last I advertised in the trade papers for a situation. Mr McLeavy answered my request. He wished me to nurse his wife back to health: a task I found impossible to perform. Mrs McLeavy was dying. Had euthanasia not been against my religion I would have practised it. Instead I decided to murder her. I administered poison during the night of June the twenty-second. In the morning I found her dead and notified the authorities. I have had nothing but heartache ever since. I am sorry for my dreadful crime. (*She weeps.*)

TRUSCOTT (*looking up from his notebook*). Very good. Your style is simple and direct. It's a theme which less skilfully handled could've given offence. (*He puts away his notebook.*) One of the most accomplished confessions I've heard in some time.

He gives MCLEAVY *a police whistle.*

I'll just arrange transport. Blow that if she should attempt to escape. My men will come to your aid immediately. The sooner we get a spoonful of Mrs McLeavy on a slide the sooner McMahon faces that murder rap.

He goes off left.

MCLEAVY (*to* FAY). How could you rob me of my only support?

FAY. I intended to provide a replacement.

MCLEAVY. I never knew such wickedness was possible.

FAY. You were aware of my character when you employed me. My references were signed by people of repute.

MCLEAVY. You murdered most of them.

FAY. That doesn't invalidate their signatures.

MCLEAVY. Pack your bags! You're not being arrested from my house.

FAY *dabs at her eyes with a handkerchief.*

DENNIS. I've never seen you in adversity. It's an unforgettable experience. I love you. I'll wait for you for ever.

FAY. No, you'll tire of waiting and marry someone else.

HAL. He won't be able to. (*He runs his hand along the coffin lid.*) Not when the Inspector asks to see mum's remains. He'll have us by the short hairs, baby.

TRUSCOTT *re-enters left with* MEADOWS.

TRUSCOTT. We're ready when you are, McMahon.

FAY *holds out her hand to* HAL. HAL *shakes it and kisses her.*

HAL (*kissing* FAY'S *hand*). Good-bye. I count a mother well lost to have met you.

DENNIS *kisses* FAY'S *hand.*

DENNIS. I shall write to you. We're allowed one letter a week.

FAY. How sweet you are. I'd like to take you both to prison with me.

TRUSCOTT. They'd certainly do more good in Holloway than you will. Take her away, Meadows.

MEADOWS *approaches* FAY *with the handcuffs. She holds out her hands.* MEADOWS *hesitates, bends swiftly and kisses* FAY'S *hand.*

Meadows!

MEADOWS *handcuffs* FAY, *and leads her out.*

Nothing but a miracle can save her now.

MEADOWS *goes off with* FAY.

(*To* MCLEAVY). I understand your wife is embalmed, sir?

MCLEAVY. Yes.

TRUSCOTT. It's a delicate subject, sir, but for the post-mortem we shall want Mrs McLeavy's stomach. Where are you keeping it?

MCLEAVY. In the little casket.

TRUSCOTT. Where is it?

HAL. In the hall.

TRUSCOTT. Fetch it, will you?

HAL *goes off left.*

DENNIS. I have something to say which will be a shock to you, Inspector.

TRUSCOTT (*nodding, taking out his pipe*). What is it? Tell it to your uncle (*He smiles.*)

DENNIS. After I'd reached the coffin I went back for the little casket. As I reached it a violent explosion occurred. The lid of the casket was forced open and the contents dispersed.

HAL *enters left. He carries the casket. He turns it upside down. The hinged lid swings free.*

It's well known in the trade that the viscera, when heated, is an unstable element.

HAL. The contents of my mother's stomach have been destroyed.

TRUSCOTT *shakes his head, bowled over.*

TRUSCOTT. What an amazing woman McMahon is. She's got away with it again. She must have influence with Heaven.

HAL. God is a gentleman. He prefers blondes.

TRUSCOTT. Call her back! Look sharp! She'll sue us for wrongful arrest.

HAL *and* DENNIS *go off left.*

MCLEAVY (*to* TRUSCOTT). I'm sorry, sir, but I'm rather confused as to what has been said and in answer to whom.

TRUSCOTT. Briefly, sir, without your wife's stomach we have no evidence on which to convict.

MCLEAVY. Can't you do a reconstruction job on my wife's insides.

TRUSCOTT. Even God can't work miracles, sir.

MCLEAVY. Is the world mad? Tell me it's not.

TRUSCOTT. I'm not paid to quarrel with accepted facts.

FAY *enters with* HAL *and* DENNIS.

Well, McMahon, you've had another twelfth-hour escape?

FAY. Yes. I shall spend a quiet hour with my rosary after tea.

MCLEAVY (*to* FAY). I know one thing, you'll be black-listed. I'll see you never get another nursing job.

TRUSCOTT. There's no need to be vindictive. Show a little tolerance.

MCLEAVY. Is she going to get away with murder?

TRUSCOTT. I'm afraid so, sir. However, I've an ace up my sleeve. The situation for law and order, though difficult, is by no means hopeless. There's still a chance, albeit a slim one, that I can get McMahon as accessory to another crime. And one which the law regards as far more serious than the taking of human life.

MCLEAVY. What's more serious than mass murder?

TRUSCOTT. Stealing public money. And that is just what your son and his accomplices have done.

MCLEAVY. Harold would never do a thing like that. He belongs to the Sons of Divine Providence.

TRUSCOTT. That may make a difference to Divine Providence, but it cuts no ice with me.

He takes the eye from his pocket.

During the course of my investigations I came across this object. Could you explain to me what it is?

He hands the eye to MCLEAVY.

MCLEAVY (*examining it*). It's a marble.

TRUSCOTT. No. Not a marble. (*He regards* MCLEAVY *calmly.*) It looks suspiciously to me like an eye. The question I'd like answered is – to whom does it legally belong?

MCLEAVY. I'm not sure that it is an eye. I think it's a marble which has been trod on.

TRUSCOTT. It's an eye, sir. (*He takes the eye from* MCLEAVY.) The makers' name is clearly marked: J. & S. Frazer, Eye-makers to the Profession.

FAY. It's mine. My father left it to me in his will.

TRUSCOTT. That's a strange bequest for a father to make.

FAY. I always admired it. It's said to have belonged originally to a well-loved figure of the concert platform.

TRUSCOTT. You're a clever woman, McMahon. Unfortunately you're not quite clever enough. I'm no fool.

FAY. Your secret is safe with me.

TRUSCOTT. I've a shrewd suspicion where this eye came from. (*He smiles.*) You know too, don't you?

FAY. No.

TRUSCOTT. Don't lie to me! It's from your sewing dummy, isn't it?

FAY (*laughing*). It's no good, Inspector. You're too clever by half.

TRUSCOTT. I'm glad you've decided to tell the truth at last. We must return the eye to its rightful owner. Unwrap the dummy.

FAY. No, no! You can't undress her in front of four men. I must do it in private.

MCLEAVY. One moment. (*To* TRUSCOTT.) Let me see that eye.

TRUSCOTT *gives it to him.*

(*To* FAY.) Who gave you this?

FAY. It's from my dummy. Didn't you hear the Inspector?

MCLEAVY (*to* TRUSCOTT). Is it likely they'd fit eyes to a sewing machine? Does that convince you?

TRUSCOTT. Nothing ever convinces me. I choose the least unlikely explanation and file it in our records.

MCLEAVY (*to* FAY). Who gave you this? Come on now!

DENNIS. I gave it to her. A woman gave it to me as a souvenir.

MCLEAVY. Of what?

DENNIS. A special occasion.

MCLEAVY. It must've been a very special occasion if she gave you her eye to mark it. Come along, I'm not the police. I want a sensible answer. Who gave it to you?

HAL. I did.

MCLEAVY (*shrieks*). You! Oh, Sacred Heaven, no!

TRUSCOTT. We're open to serious discussion, sir, but not bad language.

MCLEAVY. This is stolen property. This eye belongs to my wife.

TRUSCOTT. On what do you base your assumption?

MCLEAVY. My wife had glass eyes.

TRUSCOTT. A remarkable woman, sir. How many were in her possession at the time of her death?

MCLEAVY. None.

TRUSCOTT. I see.

MCLEAVY. These were fitted after death. Her own were taken away.

TRUSCOTT. Where to?

MCLEAVY. I don't know.

TRUSCOTT. Did you never think to inquire?

MCLEAVY. No.

TRUSCOTT. You act in a singularly heartless manner for someone who claims to have been happily married.

MCLEAVY. Oh, Inspector – (*Brokenly*) – my son, you heard
him confess it, has stolen the eyes from the dead; a practice
unknown outside of medical science. I have reared a ghoul at
my own expense.

Silence. TRUSCOTT *considers.*

TRUSCOTT. What do you wish me to do, sir?

MCLEAVY. Fetch a screwdriver. The coffin must be opened. I
want to know what else thievery stoops to. Her head may
have gone as well.

DENNIS. Might I advise caution, Mr McLeavy? From a pro-
fessional point of view? The coffin took a pasting, you know.

FAY. She may be in pieces.

MCLEAVY. Fetch a screwdriver.

HAL. Couldn't we bury the eye separately?

MCLEAVY. I can't ask the priest to hold the burial service over
an eye. Fetch a screwdriver.

Nobody moves. TRUSCOTT *draws a deep breath.*

TRUSCOTT. What good will it do, sir?

MCLEAVY. I'm not interested in doing good. There are or-
ganizations devoted to that purpose. Fetch a screwdriver!
Do I have to repeat it like the muezzin?

DENNIS *gives* MCLEAVY *a screwdriver.* MCLEAVY *hands
the eye to* TRUSCOTT *and begins to unscrew the coffin lid.*

TRUSCOTT. This is unwarranted interference with the rights of
the dead. As a policeman I must ask you to consider your
actions most carefully.

MCLEAVY. She's my wife. I can do what I like with her. Anything is legal with a corpse.

TRUSCOTT. Indeed it is not. Conjugal rights should stop with the last heartbeat. I thought you knew that.

MCLEAVY *begins to unscrew the second side of the coffin.*

I must say, sir, I'm aghast at this behaviour. Equivalent to tomb robbing it is. What do you hope to gain by it? An eyeless approach to Heaven is as likely to succeed as any. Your priest will confirm what I say.

MCLEAVY *bows his head, continues his work.*

You strike me, sir – I have to say this – as a thoroughly irresponsible individual. Always creating unnecessary trouble.

HAL. We'll have the house full of the law. Half our fittings will be missing. That's why they have such big pockets on their uniforms.

TRUSCOTT. Your son seems to have a more balanced idea of the world in which we live than you do, sir.

MCLEAVY. My duty is clear.

TRUSCOTT. Only the authorities can decide when your duty is clear. Wild guesses by persons like yourself can only cause confusion.

MCLEAVY *lifts the coffin lid.*

HAL. He's going to be shocked. See him preparing for it. His generation takes a delight in being outraged.

MCLEAVY *looks into the coffin, gives a grunt of disbelief, staggers back, incredulous.*

DENNIS. Catch him! He's going to faint.

He and FAY *support* MCLEAVY *and help him to the bed.* MCLEAVY *sinks beside the corpse in a state of shock.*

MCLEAVY. Where? (*Bewildered.*) Where? (*He follows* HAL's *glance to the corpse and recoils in horror.*) Oh, the end of the world is near when such crimes are committed.

TRUSCOTT. The opening of a coffin couldn't possibly herald Armageddon. Pull yourself together, sir.

FAY (*to* TRUSCOTT). The condition of the corpse has deteriorated due to the accident. Do you wish to verify the fact?

TRUSCOTT (*shuddering*). No, thank you, miss. I receive enough shocks in the line of duty without going about looking for them.

FAY (*to* DENNIS). Replace the lid on the coffin.

DENNIS *does so.*

MCLEAVY (*to* HAL). I shall disown you. I'll publish it abroad that I was cuckolded.

FAY (*to* TRUSCOTT). It's been a harrowing experience for him.

TRUSCOTT. He was warned in advance of the consequences of his action.

HAL (*kneeling to* MCLEAVY). I'm in a bit of a spot, Dad. I don't mind confessing. Don't get stroppy with me, eh?

MCLEAVY. I'm sorry I ever got you. I'd've withheld myself at the conception if I'd known.

TRUSCOTT. Such idle fantasies ill become you, sir.

MCLEAVY *chokes back his sobs.*

Fathers have discovered greater iniquities in their sons than the theft of an eye. The episode isn't without instruction.

MCLEAVY. Where did I go wrong? His upbringing was faultless. (*To* DENNIS.) Did you lead him astray?

DENNIS. I was innocent till I met him.

HAL. You met me when you were three days old.

MCLEAVY (*to* HAL). Where are your tears? She was your mother.

HAL. It's dust, Dad.

MCLEAVY *shakes his head in despair.*

A little dust.

MCLEAVY. I loved her.

HAL. You had her filleted without a qualm. Who could have affection for a half-empty woman?

MCLEAVY (*groaning*). Oh, Jesus, Mary, Joseph, guide me to the end of my wits and have done with it.

HAL. You've lost nothing. You began the day with a dead wife. You end it with a dead wife.

MCLEAVY. Oh, wicked, wicked. (*Wildly.*) These hairs – (*Points.*) – they're grey. You made them so. I'd be a redhead today had you been an accountant.

TRUSCOTT (*removing his pipe from his mouth*). We really can't accept such unlikely explanation for the colour of your hair, sir.

> MCLEAVY *wails aloud in anguish.*

Your behaviour indicates a growing lack of control. It's disgraceful in a man of your age and background. I'm half inclined to book you for disturbing the peace.

> FAY *hands* MCLEAVY *a handkerchief. He blows his nose. He draws himself up to his full height.*

MCLEAVY. I'm sorry, Inspector. My behaviour must seem strange to you. I'll endeavour to explain it. You can then do as you think fit.

FAY. Consider the consequences of telling the truth. It will kill Father Jellicoe.

DENNIS. My pigeons will die if I'm nicked. There'll be nobody to feed them.

> Silence. TRUSCOTT *opens his notebook and looks at* MC-LEAVY.

MCLEAVY. I wish to prefer charges.

HAL (*desperate*). If my Aunt Bridie hears of this, she'll leave her money to an orphanage. You know how selfish she is.

TRUSCOTT. Whom do you wish to charge, sir?

MCLEAVY (*pause, struggles with his conscience, at last*). Myself.

TRUSCOTT (*looking up from his notebook*). What crime have you committed?

MCLEAVY. I— I— (*Sweating.*) I've given misleading information to the police.

TRUSCOTT. What information?

MCLEAVY. I told you that the eye belonged to my wife. It doesn't. (*Conscience stricken.*) Oh, God forgive me for what I'm doing.

TRUSCOTT. If the eye doesn't belong to your wife, to whom does it belong?

> MCLEAVY *is unable to answer; he stares about him, perplexed.*

FAY (*with a smile*). It belongs to my sewing dummy, Inspector. Your original deduction was quite correct.

> TRUSCOTT *slowly puts away his notebook and pencil.*

TRUSCOTT. I ought to have my head examined, getting mixed up in a case of this kind. (*To* MCLEAVY.) Your conduct is scandalous, sir. With you for a father this lad never stood a chance. No wonder he took to robbing banks.

MCLEAVY (*in shame*). What are you going to do?

TRUSCOTT. Do? I'm going to leave this house at once. I've never come across such people. You behave as though you're affiliated to Bedlam.

MCLEAVY. But – the bank robbery – is the case closed?

TRUSCOTT. No, sir, it's not closed. We don't give up as easily as that. I'm going to have this place turned upside down.

MCLEAVY. Oh, dear, what a nuisance. And in a house of mourning, too.

TRUSCOTT. Your wife won't be here, sir. I shall take possession of the remains.

FAY. Why do you need the remains? You can't prove Mrs McLeavy was murdered.

TRUSCOTT. There's no cause for alarm. It's a mere formality.

You're quite safe. (*He smiles. To* MCLEAVY.) There's no one more touchy than your hardened criminal. (*He puts his pipe away.*) I'll be back in ten minutes. And then, I'm afraid, a lot of damage will be done to your property. You'll be paying repair bills for months to come. One unfortunate suspect recently had the roof taken off his house.

MCLEAVY. Isn't there anything I can do to prevent this appalling assault upon my privacy?

TRUSCOTT. Well, sir, if you can suggest a possible hiding-place for the money?

> MCLEAVY *hangs his head.*

MCLEAVY (*almost in a whisper*). I can't, Inspector.

TRUSCOTT. Very well. You must take the consequences of ignorance. (*He tips his hat.*) I'll be back soon.

> *He goes off left.*

MCLEAVY. Oh, what a terrible thing I've done. I've obstructed an officer in the course of his duty.

HAL (*hugging him*). I'm proud of you. I'll never feel ashamed of bringing my friends home now.

MCLEAVY. I shan't be able to face my reflection in the mirror.

FAY. Go to confession. Book an hour with Father Mac.

HAL. Oh, not him! Three brandies and he's away. The barmaid at the King of Denmark is blackmailing half the district.

MCLEAVY. I'll say nothing of what I've discovered if you return the money to the bank. You're not to keep a penny of it. Do you understand?

HAL. Yes, Dad. (*He winks at* DENNIS.)

MCLEAVY. I'll go and ring Father Jellicoe. My soul is in torment.

> MCLEAVY *goes off left.*

HAL (*closing the door, to* FAY). Unwrap the body. Once we've got it back into the coffin we're home and dry.

FAY *pulls the screen round the bed. She goes behind the screen to unwrap the corpse.*

DENNIS. What are we going to do with the money?

HAL. Put in into the casket.

DENNIS. Won't he want that?

HAL. He knows it's empty.

DENNIS *takes the lid from the coffin.*

DENNIS. Why didn't we put it in there in the first place?

HAL. My mum's guts were in there. The damp would've got at the notes.

HAL *opens the casket.*

Got a hanky?

DENNIS *throws a handkerchief over.* HAL *wipes the inside of the casket.*

DENNIS. Oh, you've gone too far! Using my handkerchief for that. It was a birthday present.

HAL *throws him the handkerchief back.*

HAL. Relax, baby. You'll have other birthdays.

DENNIS *throws the bundles of notes to* HAL. HAL *packs them into the casket.*

I shall accompany my father to Confession this evening. In order to purge my soul of this afternoon's events.

DENNIS. It's at times like this that I regret not being a Catholic.

HAL. Afterwards I'll take you to a remarkable brothel I've found. Really remarkable. Run by three Pakistanis aged between ten and fifteen. They do it for sweets. Part of their religion. Meet me at seven. Stock up with Mars bars.

FAY *appears from behind the screen, folding the mattress cover.*

FAY. Don't look behind there, Harold.

HAL. Why not?

FAY. Your mother is naked.

She hangs the folded cover over the screen.
HAL *packs the last bundle of notes into the casket.*

HAL. We're safe.

He bangs down the lid.

Nobody will ever look in there.

TRUSCOTT *enters left.*

TRUSCOTT. I've fixed everything to my satisfaction. My men
will be here shortly. They're perfectly capable of causing
damage unsupervised, and so I shall take my leave of you.
(*He bows, smiles.*)

FAY (*shaking hands*). Good-bye, Inspector. It's been nice meet-
ing you again.

TRUSCOTT. Good-bye. (*He nods to* HAL *and* DENNIS.) I'd
better take the little casket with me.

HAL. It's empty!

TRUSCOTT. I must have it certified empty before I close my
report.

FAY. We're having it de-sanctified. Mr McLeavy is on the
phone to the priest about it.

TRUSCOTT. Our lads in forensic aren't interested in sanctity.
Give me that casket!

MCLEAVY *enters left. He sees* TRUSCOTT *and cowers back.*

MCLEAVY. You're back already? Have you decided to arrest
me after all?

TRUSCOTT. I wouldn't arrest you if you were the last man on
earth. (*To* HAL.) Give me that casket! (*He takes the casket
from* HAL. *To* MCLEAVY.) I'll give you a receipt, sir.

He looks for somewhere to rest the casket, sees the empty coffin puts the casket down.

Where is Mrs McLeavy?

FAY. She's behind the screen.

TRUSCOTT *looks behind the screen and raises his eyebrows.*

TRUSCOTT. Did she ask to be buried like that?

MCLEAVY. Yes.

TRUSCOTT. She was a believer in that sort of thing?

MCLEAVY. Yes.

TRUSCOTT. Are you, sir?

MCLEAVY. Well no. I'm not a member myself.

TRUSCOTT. A member? She belonged to a group, then?

MCLEAVY. Oh, yes. They met a couple of times a week. They do a lot of good for the country. Raising money for charities, holding fetes. The old folk would be lost without them.

TRUSCOTT. I've heard many excuses for nudists, sir, but never that one.

MCLEAVY (*pause*). Nudists?

TRUSCOTT. Your wife was a nudist, you say?

MCLEAVY. My wife never took her clothes off in public in her life.

TRUSCOTT. Yet she asked to be buried in that condition?

MCLEAVY. What condition?

TRUSCOTT. In the nude.

MCLEAVY (*with dignity*). You'd better leave my house, Inspector. I can't allow you to insult the memory of my late wife.

TRUSCOTT (*tearing a sheet of paper from his notebook*). You give me a lot of aggravation, sir. Really you do. (*He hands the paper to* MCLEAVY.) You'll get your property back in due course.

He lifts casket, the lid swings away and the bundles of bank-notes fall to the floor. TRUSCOTT *stares at the notes scattered at his feet in silence.*

Who is responsible for this disgraceful state of affairs?

HAL. I am.

TRUSCOTT (*stoops and picks up a bundle of notes*). Would you have stood by and allowed this money to be buried in holy ground?

HAL. Yes.

TRUSCOTT. How dare you involve me in a situation for which no memo has been issued. (*He turns the notes over.*) In all my experience I've never come across a case like it. Every one of these fivers bears a portrait of the Queen. It's dreadful to contemplate the issues raised. Twenty thousand tiaras and twenty thousand smiles buried alive! She's a constitutional monarch, you know. She can't answer back.

DENNIS. Will she send us a telegram?

TRUSCOTT. I'm sure she will.

He picks up another bundle and stares at them.

MCLEAVY. Well, Inspector, you've found the money and unmasked the criminals. You must do your duty and arrest them. I shall do mine and appear as witness for the prosecution.

HAL. Are you married, Inspector?

TRUSCOTT. Yes.

HAL. Does your wife never yearn for excitement?

TRUSCOTT. She did once express a wish to see the windmills and tulip fields of Holland.

HAL. With such an intelligent wife you need a larger income.

TRUSCOTT. I never said my wife was intelligent.

HAL. Then she's unintelligent? Is that it?

TRUSCOTT. My wife is a woman. Intelligence doesn't really enter into the matter.

HAL. If, as you claim, your wife is a woman, you certainly need a larger income.

TRUSCOTT *takes his pipe from his pocket and sticks it into the corner of his mouth.*

TRUSCOTT. Where is this Jesuitical twittering leading us?

HAL. I'm about to suggest bribery.

TRUSCOTT *removes his pipe, no one speaks.*

TRUSCOTT. How much?

HAL. Twenty per cent.

TRUSCOTT. Twenty-five per cent. Or a full report of this case appears on my superior officer's desk in the morning.

HAL. Twenty-five it is.

TRUSCOTT (*shaking hands*). Done.

DENNIS (*to* TRUSCOTT). May I help you to replace the money in the casket?

TRUSCOTT. Thank you, lad. Most kind of you.

DENNIS *packs the money into the casket.* FAY *takes* MRS MCLEAVY'S *clothes from the bedpan on the invalid chair and goes behind the screen.* TRUSCOTT *chews on his pipe.* HAL *and* DENNIS *take the coffin behind the screen.*

MCLEAVY. Has no one considered my feelings in all this?

TRUSCOTT. What percentage do you want?

MCLEAVY. I don't want money. I'm an honest man.

TRUSCOTT. You'll have to mend your ways then.

MCLEAVY. I shall denounce the lot of you!

TRUSCOTT. Now then, sir, be reasonable. What has just taken place is perfectly scandalous and had better go no farther than these three walls. It's not expedient for the general public to have its confidence in the police force undermined. You'd be doing the community a grave disservice by revealing the full frightening facts of this case.

MCLEAVY. What kind of talk is that? You don't make sense.

TRUSCOTT. Who does?

MCLEAVY. I'll go to the priest. He makes sense. He makes sense to me.

TRUSCOTT. Does he make sense to himself? That is much more important.

MCLEAVY. If I can't trust the police, I can still rely on the Fathers. They'll advise me what to do!

He goes off left. HAL *appears from behind the screen.*

HAL. You'll be glad to know that my mother is back in her last resting-place.

TRUSCOTT. Good. You've carried out the operation with speed and efficiency. I congratulate you.

DENNIS *appears from behind the screen.*

DENNIS. We're ready for the eye now. If you'd like to assist us.

TRUSCOTT (*taking the eye from his pocket*). You do it, lad. You're more experienced in these matters than me.

He hands DENNIS *the eye.*

HAL. You'd better have these as well.

He hands DENNIS *the teeth.*
DENNIS *takes the eye and teeth behind the screen.*

TRUSCOTT. Your sense of detachment is terrifying, lad. Most people would at least flinch upon seeing their mother's eyes and teeth handed around like nuts at Christmas.

FAY *appears from behind the screen.*

FAY. Have you given a thought to the priest?

TRUSCOTT. We can't have him in on it, miss. Our percentage wouldn't be worth having.

FAY. Mr McLeavy has threatened to expose us.

TRUSCOTT. I've been exposed before.

FAY. What happened?

TRUSCOTT. I arrested the man. He's doing twelve years.

HAL. If you wish to arrest my dad, you'll find me an exemplary witness.

TRUSCOTT. What a bright idea. We've vacancies in the force for lads of your calibre. (*To* FAY.) Are you with us, McMahon?

FAY. Yes, it seems the best solution for all of us.

DENNIS folds up the screen. The coffin is lying on the bed.

TRUSCOTT (*to* DENNIS). And you?

DENNIS. I've never seen the view from the witness box. It'll be a new experience.

The door left bursts open. MCLEAVY *enters with* MEADOWS.

MCLEAVY (*pointing to* TRUSCOTT). This is the man. Arrest him.

TRUSCOTT. Good afternoon, Meadows. Why have you left your post?

MEADOWS. I was accosted by this man, sir. He insisted that I accompany him to the Catholic church.

TRUSCOTT. What did you say?

MEADOWS. I refused.

TRUSCOTT. Quite rightly. You're a Methodist. Proceed with the statement.

MEADOWS. The man became offensive, sir. He made a number of derogatory remarks about the force in general and yourself in particular. I called for assistance.

TRUSCOTT. Excellent, Meadows. I shall see H.Q. hear of this. You have apprehended, in full flight, a most dangerous criminal. As you know, we've had our eye upon this house for some time. I was about to unmask the chief offender when this man left the room on some excuse and disappeared.

MEADOWS. He was making a bolt for it, sir.

TRUSCOTT. You have the matter in a nutshell, Meadows. Put the cuffs on him.

MEADOWS handcuffs MCLEAVY.

You're fucking nicked, my old beauty. You've found to your cost that the standards of the British police force are as high as ever.

MCLEAVY. What am I charged with?

TRUSCOTT. That needn't concern you for the moment. We'll fill in the details later.

MCLEAVY. You can't do this. I've always been a law-abiding citizen. The police are for the protection of ordinary people.

TRUSCOTT. I don't know where you pick up these slogans, sir. You must read them on hoardings.

MCLEAVY. I want to see someone in authority.

TRUSCOTT. I am in authority. You can see me.

MCLEAVY. Someone higher.

TRUSCOTT. You can see whoever you like, providing you convince me first that you're justified in seeing them.

MCLEAVY. You're mad!

TRUSCOTT. Nonsense. I had a check-up only yesterday. Our medical officer assured me that I was quite sane.

MCLEAVY. I'm innocent. (*A little unsure of himself, the beginnings of panic.*) Doesn't that mean anything to you?

TRUSCOTT. You know the drill, Meadows. Empty his pockets and book him.

MCLEAVY *is dragged away by* MEADOWS.

MCLEAVY. I'm innocent! I'm innocent! (*At the door, pause, a last wail.*) Oh, what a terrible thing to happen to a man who's been kissed by the Pope.

MEADOWS *goes off with* MCLEAVY.

DENNIS. What will you charge him with, Inspector?

TRUSCOTT. Oh, anything will do.

FAY. Can an accidental death be arranged?

TRUSCOTT. Anything can be arranged in prison.

HAL. Except pregnancy.

TRUSCOTT. Well, of course, the chaperon system defeats us there.

He picks up the casket.

The safest place for this is in my locker at the station. It's a maxim of the force: 'Never search your own backyard – you may find what you're looking for.' (*He turns in the doorway, the casket under his arm.*) Give me a ring this evening. I should have news for you of McLeavy by then. (*He hands a card to* FAY.) This is my home address. I'm well known there.

He nods, smiles, and goes off left. Sound of front door slamming. Pause.

HAL (*with a sigh*). He's a nice man. Self-effacing in his way.

DENNIS. He has an open mind. In direct contrast to the usual run of civil servant.

HAL and DENNIS lift the coffin from the bed and place it on the trestles.

HAL. It's comforting to know that the police can still be relied upon when we're in trouble.

They stand beside the coffin, FAY *in the middle.*

FAY. We'll bury your father with your mother. That will be nice for him, won't it?

She lifts her rosary and bows her head in prayer.

HAL (*pause, to* DENNIS). You can kip here, baby. Plenty of room now. Bring your bags over tonight.

FAY *looks up.*

FAY (*sharply*). When Dennis and I are married we'd have to move out.

HAL. Why?

FAY. People would talk. We must keep up appearances.

She returns to her prayers, her lips move silently. DENNIS *and* HAL *at either side of the coffin.*

Curtain

Author's note on the first edition

The Lord Chamberlain grants a licence to the play subject to the following conditions:

(i) The corpse is inanimate and not played by an actress.

(ii) On page 79 the casket is wiped with a handkerchief. The Lord Chamberlain is particularly anxious that no stain shall appear on the handkerchief.

The following alterations to the text are required:

Act One: Page 21 'Run by a woman who was connected with the Royal Family one time.' For 'Royal Family' substitute 'Empire Loyalists'.

Page 22 'Under that picture of the Sacred Heart.' For 'Sacred Heart' substitute 'Infant Samuel'.

Page 36 'While Jesus pointed to his Sacred Heart, you pointed to yours. I never point. It's rude' must be cut.

Page 39 For 'Consummatum Est' substitute 'Kingdom Come'.

Page 51 For 'buggery' substitute 'beggary'.

Act Two: Page 79 'Run by three Pakistanis aged between ten and fifteen. They do it for sweets. Part of their religion.' For 'Pakistanis' substitute 'kids'. 'Part of their religion' must be cut.

Page 85 For 'fucking' substitute 'bleeding'.

Methuen's Modern Plays

EDITED BY JOHN CULLEN

* * *

Methuen's Theatre Classics

THE GOVERNMENT INSPECTOR	Gogol *an English version by Edward O. Marsh and Jeremy Brooks*
BRAND	Ibsen
THE WILD DUCK	*translated by Michael Meyer*
HEDDA GABLER	
THE MASTER BUILDER	
MISS JULIE	Strindberg *translated by Michael Meyer*
LADY WINDERMERE'S FAN	Wilde
THE IMPORTANCE OF BEING EARNEST	
THE PLAYBOY OF THE WESTERN WORLD	Synge

*   *   *

Methuen Playscripts

Paul Ableman	*Tests*
Barry Bermange	*Nathan and Tabileth* and *Oldenburg*
Edward Bond	*Saved*
Kenneth H. Brown	*The Brig*
David Campton	*Little brother: little sister* and *Out of the flying pan*
Henry Chapman	*You won't always be on top*
David Cregan	*Three Men for Colverton* *Transcending* and *The Dancers*
John McGrath	*Events while guarding the Bofors gun*
David Mercer	*The Governor's Lady*
Georges Michel	*The Sunday walk*
Rodney Milgate	*A refined look at existence*
Guillaume Oyono-Mbia	*Three suitors: one husband* and *Until further notice*

David Selbourne	*The play of William Cooper and Edmund Dew-Nevett*
Johnny Speight	*If there weren't any blacks you'd have to invent them*
Lanford Wilson	*Home Free!* and *The Madness of Lady Bright*

*   *   *

Other Plays from Methuen

Jean Anouilh	*Collected Plays Volume I* (The Ermine, Thieves' Carnival, Restless Heart, Traveller without Luggage, Dinner with the Family) *Collected Plays Volume II* (Time Remembered, Point of Departure, Antigone, Romeo and Jeannette, Medea)
Max Frisch	*Three Plays* (The Fire Raisers, Count Oederland, Andorra)
Jean Giraudoux	*Plays Volume I* (Tiger at the Gates, Duel of Angels, Judith) *Plays Volume II* (Amphitryon, Intermezzo, Ondine)
John Millington Synge	*Plays and Poems*